Twayne's United States Authors Series

EDITOR OF THIS VOLUME

David J. Nordloh

Indiana University

Horatio Alger, Jr.

TUSAS 363

Horatio Alger, Jr.

HORATIO ALGER, JR.

By GARY SCHARNHORST

University of Texas at Dallas

TWAYNE PUBLISHERS
A DIVISION OF G. K. HALL & CO., BOSTON

Published in 1980 by Twayne Publishers,
A Division of G. K. Hall & Co.
All Rights Reserved

Printed on permanent/durable acid-free paper and bound
in the United States of America

First Printing

Library of Congress Cataloging in Publication Data

Scharnhorst, Gary.
Horatio Alger, Jr.

(Twayne's United States authors series;
TUSAS 363)
Bibliography: p. 162-66
Includes index.
1.   Alger, Horatio, 1832-1899—Criticism and
interpretation.
PS1029.A3Z83   813'.4   80-10570
ISBN 0-8057-7252-9

To Sandy,
who, though not a banker's daughter,
I would save from drowning,
if I could swim.

Contents

About the Author

Gary Scharnhorst received the Ph.D. degree in American Studies from Purdue University and during 1978–79 served as a Fulbright lecturer at Stuttgart University in West Germany. He presently teaches in the School of Arts and Humanities at the University of Texas at Dallas. He has contributed numerous essays, including ones on Alger and the idea of success in America, to such journals as *American Quarterly*, the *Fitzgerald/Hemingway Annual*, and *American Literary Realism*.

Preface

This study attempts to trace the evolution of the idea of success in the writings of Horatio Alger, Jr., whose career as an author of juvenile fiction between the Civil War and the end of the nineteenth century roughly coincides with that period in America's history known as the Gilded Age. In a hundred and three juvenile books, eight other volumes, and scores of tales and short essays, Alger allegedly exerted an influence upon the popular American imagination far out of proportion to his slight talent as a writer. In 1937, for example, Samuel Eliot Morison and Henry Steele Commager claimed in their monumental *The Growth of the American Republic* that Alger, as well as obscure sentimentalist Martha Finley, influenced American culture more than any other author they examined, excepting only Mark Twain.[1] Similarly, Frederick Lewis Allen in 1952 suggested that Alger played a more prominent role in shaping the attitudes of American businessmen than "all the professors of economics put together."[2] In 1955, Kenneth S. Lynn hailed Alger as "one of the great mythmakers of the modern world."[3] It is noteworthy, however, that all claims regarding Alger's broad cultural influence date from the mid-twentieth century, long after Alger's works were published, sold, and popularly read. In other words, Alger's name and his "myth" have obtained an inflated, popular, modern currency with only slight reference to the man and to the books themselves. Unlike that modern "Horatio Alger" who was a best-selling hack writer of juvenile stories about boys who rise "from rags to riches," the historical Horatio Alger was a Harvard-educated patrician whose moderately popular nineteenth-century morality tracts for boys expressed his genteel abhorrence of the mercenary Gilded Age.

One of the reasons Alger's standard success story has been distorted in recent decades is that his fiction has not been read in the light of accurate biographical information. The account of how and why the five previous biographies of Alger came to be written would make an interesting story in itself—a more interesting one, perhaps, than the actual story of Alger's rather dull life. By now, most interested observers know that Herbert R. Mayes, Alger's first biographer, published in 1928 a debunking version of Alger's life and, deliberately or not, hoaxed encyclopedia makers and scholars for over forty years. This fictionalized account of Alger's life depicted the author as a neurotic obsessed with a sense of failure who consequently created his success mythology to compensate for his own personal inadequacies. Unfortunately, this biography, which became in the year of its publication the source for the Alger vita in the *Dictionary of American Biography* and, ordained by that canon, a basis for all subsequent biographies of Alger, has served to reinforce the view that Alger thematically celebrated conventional economic success in his fiction and thus was an apologist for the "Robber Barons" whom he apparently envied. The other major version of the "facts" about Alger's life, increasingly accepted in the last decade by the scholarly community as accurate and exhaustive, Ralph Gardner's *Horatio Alger, or The American Hero Era* (1964), unfortunately is not only avowedly apologetic toward its subject but incomplete, and padded with incidents and their "documentation" which Gardner apparently invented to entertain the book collectors for whom he was writing. Not only did Gardner ignore the evidence of Alger's homosexuality (an omission, incidentally, which Edwin P. Hoyt tries to remedy in the extreme in his sensational and faddish *Horatio's Boys* [1974], a biography which otherwise is a mere rewrite of Gardner's) but he also failed to examine numerous documents known to exist at the time he wrote his book. Hoyt's supposedly complete work merely compounds the problem, for by deferring to Gardner in most biographical matters, he leaves the impression that virtually all possible light has been shed on Alger's life. Such is not the case. For example, Gardner in his volume, and Hoyt following his lead, describe Alger's relationships with some of the leading men and women of letters during the late nineteenth century, among them Harriet Beecher Stowe, Mark Twain, and Bret Harte. These quaint renderings in effect suggest that Alger lived at least on the fringes of a community of artists, considered himself an artist, and was accepted by others as one. Such a pretty picture is, however, a blatant fabrication. Not a scrap of extant evidence confirms that Alger ever so much as talked with any of these individuals personally; indeed, it appears as though some eminent writers whom he did know personally, such as Henry James, deliberately and carefully shunned him.

To correct these versions of the Alger biography and the psychoanalytic or apologetic interpretations of his stories which they feed, as well as to provide a reliable cultural context in which Alger's work may be set, the first two chapters of this study offer a biography that views Alger as a product of his culture. This treatment of Alger's life and work, the first book about Alger to be fully documented, is based entirely on reliable and authoritative sources, including not only all documents used by Gardner and Hoyt, but several additional ones. Gardner and Hoyt, for example, examined about a hundred letters written by Alger, and over eighty of those were written to a single correspondent over a brief, five-year period. This study profits from reference to over a hundred and sixty letters, still a meager number, but many of the additional ones offer new information and fresh insight into Alger's life. Some information which may seem entirely superfluous and inconsequential to the general reader has been included in these chapters simply to correct the erroneous details invented by previous biographers.

I for one do not claim that Alger's life is a particularly interesting or representative one, nor that his writing has much merit. Indeed, I am willing to admit that were Alger's name not associated with the rags-to-riches hero of American myth, were the phrase "Horatio Alger hero" not in the popular currency, his life and work, like that of his long-forgotten friend and colleague Oliver Optic, would command little more than passing attention. But because his name has become a metaphor of economic success in America, because the purpose and plot of his formulaic fiction have become distorted during the generations he has remained unread, because he is considered important by so many who invoke his name and supposed authority, it is important both to set straight the record of his life and to establish clearly what and for what purpose he did write. Chapters 3, 4, and 5, then, analyze Alger's fiction—both that for adults and that for juveniles—in light of his didactic purpose. In short, this study "de-mythologizes" Alger and reinterprets his work in order to frame the more significant and difficult problem of how a nineteenth-century writer of moderately popular morality tracts whose appeal was essentially nostalgic came to be considered in the twentieth century an apologist for industrial capitalism and a celebrant of mercenary values and business acumen who genuflected at the altar of the bitch-goddess Success. Although such a limited study as this one cannot offer a complete answer to the question, it does point in chapter 6 in what may be a promising direction.

I am indebted to Professors Chester E. Eisinger, Cheryl Oreovicz, and Lester Cohen for patient criticism of most of the material in this volume and to Professor Charles White for timely encouragement. Alger enthusiasts Jack Bales, Gilbert K. Westgard II, Rohima Walter, Bob Bennett, and Dick Seddon all provided helpful advice and, in several cases, copies of Alger correspondence in their personal collections. Although they each may differ from my own assessment of Alger in this work, their assistance is deeply appreciated. I wish also to acknowledge the assistance of Indiana University, which offered me a Lilly Library Fellowship for the purpose of doing research of the kind I describe in chapter 6, and the following institutions, all of which provided copies of Alger letters: Henry E. Huntington Library; Beinecke Rare Book and Manuscript Library, Yale University, Library of Congress; University of Iowa; Knox College Archives; Houghton Library and University Archives, Harvard University; American Antiquarian Society; William L. Clements Library, University of Michigan; Butler Library, Columbia University; Haverford College; Charles Patterson Van Pelt Library, University of Pennsylvania; Lee Library, Brigham Young University; New York Public Library; Phillips Exeter Academy; Illinois State Historical Society; Alderman Library, University of Virginia. Mrs. Harriet Stratemeyer Adams also kindly granted me permission to use letters that Alger wrote to her father, Edward Stratemeyer; These letters have since been housed in the private archives of the Stratemeyer Syndicate, Maplewood, New Jersey.

GARY F. SCHARNHORST

University of Texas at Dallas

Chronology

ca.   Thomas Alger immigrated from England to near Taunton,
1665   Massachusetts.

1829– Horatio Alger, father of the writer, graduated from Cam-
1831   bridge Divinity School, married Olive Augusta Fenno, and
       settled over the Unitarian Society of Chelsea, Massachusetts.

1832   January 13, Horatio Alger, Jr., born, Chelsea, Massachu-
       setts.

1844   The elder Horatio Alger defaulted on debts. Family moved
       to Marlborough, Massachusetts.

1844– Alger, Jr., attended Gates Academy, Marlborough, in prep-
1847   aration for admission to Harvard College.

1848– Attended Harvard, graduating eighth in his class. Member
1852   of Phi Beta Kappa.

1849   First publications appeared in a nationally distributed mag-
       azine, the *Pictorial National Library*.

1851   Awarded Bowdoin Prize at Harvard.

1852– Worked at a variety of teaching, writing, and editing jobs in
1857   New England.

1856   *Bertha's Christmas Vision: An Autumn Sheaf*, Alger's first
       published volume, appeared.

1857– Published stories and poems in *Harper's* and *Putnam's*.
1858

1857– Attended Cambridge Divinity School while writing.
1860

1860– First trip to Europe.
1861

1861– Resided in Cambridge while teaching and writing.
1864

1863   Published essay in *North American Review* on funeral of
       Eugene Scribe.

1864   Published *Frank's Campaign*, his first juvenile fiction and
       first volume in the three-volume "Campaign series."

1864– Minister of the Unitarian Society of Brewster, Massachu-
1866   setts. Contributed "a large number of stories and poems" to
       Harper's Weekly.

1866 Dismissed from Brewster pulpit. *Timothy Crump's Ward,*
      Helen Ford, "John Maynard."
1866– Resided in New York and wrote nearly a hundred juvenile
1896 novels.
1867– Serialization and first book publication of *Ragged Dick,* Al-
1868 ger's most popular work and only best seller during his life.
1868– "Ragged Dick series" of eight volumes, including *Mark the*
1871 *Match Boy* and *Ben the Luggage Boy.*
1869– Tutored the sons of the banker Joseph Seligman.
1881
1870 Began collaboration with William Rounseville Alger on *Life*
      of Edwin Forrest.
1871– "Tattered Tom series" of eight volumes, including *Phil the*
1879 *Fiddler, The Young Outlaw,* and *Julius.*
1871– "Luck and Pluck series" of eight volumes, including *Bound*
1875 *to Rise* and *Risen from the Ranks.*
1872– "Brave and Bold series" of four volumes.
1877
1873 Second tour of Europe.
1875 *Grand'ther Baldwin's Thanksgiving.*
1876 *The New Schoolma'am, or A Summer in North Sparta.*
1877– Toured the American West to gather material for "Pacific
1878 series" of four volumes.
ca.   Completed manuscript of "Mabel Parker," a still unpub-
1878 lished adult novel.
1881 A. K. Loring, the Boston publisher of all Alger juvenile
      novels to date, declared bankruptcy.
1881– Juvenile biographies of Garfield, Lincoln, Webster.
1883
1883 Hired to tutor Benjamin Cardozo.
1883– "Atlantic series" of four juvenile novels, including *Do and*
1886 *Dare.*
1887– "Way to Success series" of four volumes, including *Strug-*
1890 *gling Upward* and *The Store Boy.*
1887– Traveled to West to gather local color material for *Luke*
1890 *Walton* and other books.
1889 "Silas Snobden's Office Boy" serialized in *Argosy.*
1890 "Are My Boys Real?" in *Ladies' Home Journal.*
1892– "New World series" of three volumes, including *Jed the*
1893 *Poorhouse Boy* and *Digging for Gold: A Story of California.*

Chronology

1893   "Cast Upon the Breakers" serialized in *Argosy*.
1893– "Rupert's Ambition" serialized in *Argosy*.
1894
1895   *The Disagreeable Woman*, Alger's final adult novel.
1896   Retired to South Natick, Massachusetts, his health broken by overwork.
1898   Arranged for Edward Stratemeyer to complete the manuscript of *Out for Business*, his final novel.
1899   June 18, died in South Natick.

CHAPTER 1

Struggling Upward

SINCE his death in 1899, Horatio Alger, Jr., has been the subject of deception and misinformation, at least in part because Alger himself shunned publicity and wished his private life to be shrouded in obscurity. His modesty may be attributed to his sincere desire to be regarded as an unobtrusive moral teacher of boys, or, related to this, his fear that details concerning his embarassing dismissal from the Unitarian pulpit in Brewster, Massachusetts, would be discovered and publicly reported. Whatever the reason for his reticence, the scanty facts about Alger's life that are available provide background necessary for an understanding of his fiction.

I Early Years

Horatio Alger, Jr., the son of a Unitarian minister, was born in Chelsea (later incorporated into Revere), Massachusetts, on January 13, 1832.[1] A seventh-generation descendant of one Thomas Alger, a British immigrant who settled near Taunton, Massachusetts, in about 1665, Alger's pedigree was a decidedly patrician one. He was distantly related to the brothers Edmund and Sylvanus Lazell, the first a member of the Constitutional Convention and the second a brigadier general in the Revolutionary Army. Alger's own paternal grandmother, Hannah Bassett Alger, was a direct descendant on her father's side of William Bassett, on her mother's side of the Reverend Robert Cushman, both of whom were among the Plymouth pilgrims. Alger's father, the elder Horatio Alger (1806–1881), graduated from Harvard College in 1825 and from Cambridge Theological School in 1829, and in September, 1829, was ordained to succeed the Reverend Dr. Joseph Tuckerman as pastor of the Unitarian Society of Chelsea, Massachusetts, where he remained until 1844. He subsequently served parishes in Marlborough and South Natick, Massachusetts, before retiring in 1874. During his ministerial career, he contributed essays of biblical commentary to the *Unitarian Advocate* and to the prestigious *Monthly Religious Magazine and Theological Review.*[2]

The elder Horatio Alger, according to all available evidence, was an impoverished man. Soon after his marriage to Olive Augusta Fenno (1807–1878) in March, 1831, and the birth ten months later of his namesake, the first of their five children, he sought to supplement his ministerial allowance by becoming, in July, 1832, the postmaster of Chelsea, serving in that office until 1842. He also represented the village in the Massachusetts legislature of 1833.[3] For several years in the late 1830s he served on the local school committee, and in fact taught briefly in the local grammar school. In 1836, moreover, he began to purchase small lots of property around Chelsea for the apparent purpose of farming them, but in the spring of 1844 he defaulted on his debts and his land was assigned, melodramatically enough, to the local squire who held the mortgage. A few months later, Alger transferred his pulpit and moved his family to Marlborough, where he was installed over the Second Congregational Society.[4] Not surprisingly, considered against this backdrop, in the juvenile fiction written years later by his son, the hero's family frequently is threatened with default and eviction from the homestead. More significantly, however, the episode offers one explanation for the younger Alger's consistent espousal of environmental reform proposals, whether as a teacher, minister, or writer. Financially insecure throughout his life, the younger Alger may have been active in reform organizations such as those for temperance and children's aid as a means of resolving his status-anxiety and establishing his genteel credentials for leadership.[5]

Upon his graduation from Harvard in 1852 at the age of twenty, Horatio Alger, Jr., described his early life in a handwritten entry in the Class Book, the only lengthy autobiographical statement that he ever prepared.[6] Because of his "delicate health"[7] as a child, as he explained,

it was deemed expedient to defer my introduction into the world of "letters." I had accordingly attained the age of six before I was initiated into the mysteries of the alphabet. From this epoch my progress was, I believe, more than ordinarily rapid. At eight years of age I commenced the study of Latin and Algebra. . . . Until the age of ten I had passed very little time

in attendance at a public school. . . . The greater part of my earlier instruction was gained at home, its regularity being much disturbed by my
father's numerous engagements. Owing to his desultory mode of instruction
my time was in a great measure at my own disposal. A considerable portion
of this was devoted to reading whatever came in my way, from Josephus'
History of the Jews and works of theology to the Arabian Nights' Enter-
tainments and the wonderful adventures of Jack the Giant Killer.

Introduced as a child to classical language, advanced mathematics,
and theology, a common curriculum for the children of the moral
elite of antebellum Massachusetts, the younger Alger was prepared
intellectually from an early age to assume an office of leadership in
the cultural bureaucracy. And in such fairy tales as "Jack the Giant
Killer," Alger was introduced to the form that juvenile literature,
including his own, assumed during this era of inner-direction.[8]

In his autobiographical narrative in the Class Book of 1852, Alger
also described his boyhood in the "pleasant town" of Marlborough
and his education preparatory to entering Harvard. The town was,
he believed, "chiefly noted for the numerous hills which on all sides
surround the main village, and its abundance of fruit trees. The
manufacture of shoes which is carried on to a considerable extent
gives a business air to what would otherwise be a quiet agricultural
town." Alger later would set dozens of juvenile novels in fictional
recreations of the pre-industrial village he recalled from his boyhood. In *Bound to Rise* (1873), for example, the hero adopts the
values of a village in antebellum Massachusetts while he earns a
little money pegging shoes in the local unmechanized factory. To
the teen-aged Alger, however, it was more important that "there
was in this place a small academy in successful operation, under the
superintendence of Mr. O. W. Albee, a graduate of Brown, and
quite a respectable scholar. . . . Though the idea had been long
entertained, now for the first time I commenced a course of study
preparatory to entering college. Beneath the elm trees in front of
Gates' Academy (for so it was called) I have conned many a lesson
in Latin, Greek, and mathematics." Completing his studies in the
Academy a year before actually entering Harvard, Alger passed the
time, "which approached as nearly to the famous *dolce far niente*
as could be desired," in the study of several modern languages,
including French.[9] In light of Alger's own classical education and
interest in modern languages, it is not surprising that dozens of the
heroes he later invented, as in *Try and Trust* (1873), *The Young*

Salesman (1894), and *Andy Grant's Pluck* (1895), study Latin and Greek, despite the apparent impracticality of facility in those languages.

II *Harvard and Literary Acquaintances*

In the autumn of 1848, at the age of sixteen, Alger entered Harvard College and thus commenced one of the most satisfying periods of his life. Probably because of his father's poverty, he was selected to be the President's Freshman, a member of the freshman class who performed official errands for President Edward Everett and in return received about forty dollars and the rent of his room that year.[10] More significantly, Alger's developing artistic sensibility probably was shaped by the mold of Unitarian moralism during these years. While his earliest published works, which remain undiscovered, appeared when he was only thirteen years old,[11] his first noteworthy works, a poem and essays on Cervantes and chivalry, appeared in the *Pictorial National Library*, a nationally distributed Boston periodical, in 1849, the year after his matriculation. After receiving the traditional Harvard award for academic excellence, the *detur digniori*, in his sophomore year, the young classical scholar

in his Junior year took the first Bowdoin prize of forty dollars for a Dissertation on "Athens in the Time of So[crat]es," the Bowdoin prize of fifteen dollars for a Greek prize composition ["The State of Athens Before the Legislation of Solon," judged by the Greek scholar C. C. Felton], and again in the Senior year a prize for Greek composition. In the Exhibition of October, 1850, he gave a Greek version from "Lacy's Address in Behalf of the Greeks," and in the Exhibition of October, 1851, a Dissertation on "The Poetry of the Troubadors." He was Class Odist on Class Day, graduated eighth in his class [of eighty-eight], and was awarded the English Oration at Commencement. He was also a member of the Phi Beta Kappa and while in college belonged to the Institute of 1770, and the Natural History Society.[12]

Alger's electives in his senior year were Greek and German.[13] In the Greek course, probably taught by Felton, he culminated his years of study of classical languages. Through the German course, almost certainly taught by Henry Wadsworth Longfellow, he apparently sought an intimacy with the instructor. After receiving in

1875 a friendly note of congratulation from Longfellow upon the publication of a volume of his Longfellow-like ballads and slight verse, Alger reminded his old mentor of an earlier occasion: "Years since when at college, I remember calling upon you with a classmate, and I shall not soon forget the kindness with which you received the two inexperienced boys whose visit might have been regarded by many as an intrusion."[14]

The earliest extant letter from Alger's pen likewise evinces his precocious interest in literature, as well as his immature attempts at ingratiation. On September 12, 1850, soon after beginning his junior year at Harvard, he wrote to James Fenimore Cooper, whom he respectfully addressed as "the first of American Novelists," to solicit his autograph. "Permit me to take this opportunity to express to you, Sir," the teen-aged Alger wrote, "the great gratification with which I have perused many of your works—more especially the Leatherstocking Series."[15] Years later, in his own novels, Alger would frequently allude to Cooper and, on occasion, model incidents in them after those in Cooper's works.

In addition to developing his interest in literature and his proficiency in languages as a Harvard student, the patrician Alger was influenced by the standard program of instruction in the humanities there. More particularly, prior to his graduation from Harvard in 1852, he was required to complete four semester courses in philosophy. In his junior year, according to the schedule in the college catalogue for his class, Alger studied major works in the tradition of Scottish "common sense" realism—Thomas Reid's *Essays on the Intellectual Powers of Man* and Dugald Stewart's *Philosophy of the Active and Moral Powers of Man*. Perhaps the most important course required of Alger as a student at Harvard, however, was the one in moral and natural philosophy which he undertook during his senior year, and which probably was taught by James Walker, the Alford Professor of Moral Philosophy from 1839 until 1853, a disciple of the Scottish Realists, editor of textbook versions of Reid's and Stewart's works, and subsequently president of Harvard from 1853 until 1860. Required reading for this capstone course included William Whewell's *Elements of Morality*, Joseph Butler's *Analogy of Religion*, and William Paley's *Evidences of Christianity*.[16]

The influence of these and similar readings upon the moral tenor of Alger's later didactic fiction should not be underestimated, as Daniel W. Howe has suggested in *The Unitarian Conscience*, a

history of Harvard moral philosophy during the first two-thirds of
the nineteenth century,

The metaphysical foundations of Harvard Unitarianism were prepared by
the Scottish common sense philosophers. The confidence with which Thomas Reid, Dugald Stewart, and their pupils solved the most perplexing
epistemological problems [i.e., the solipsism of Berkeley and the skepticism
of Hume] appealed to the intellectual leaders of eastern Massachusetts.
Like the humanists of the Renaissance, Unitarian humanists were academ-
ically oriented, and sought the cultivation of human nature within the
framework of an organized scholarly curriculum. Upon the foundation supplied by the Scots, Harvard professors were able to construct a durable
consensus, containing room for both Enlightenment aspirations and Christian principles.[17]

Heirs of the Christian Enlightenment, the Harvard Unitarians
"were confident that nature spoke to man of God, revealing a divine
order at once intellectually satisfying and morally uplifting."[18] In
the philosophy text by Bishop Butler assigned to him by his Harvard
instructor, for example, Alger would have read the following: "That
which renders beings capable of moral government, is their having
a moral nature, and moral faculties · of perception and of
action. . . . That we have this moral approving and disapproving
faculty is certain from our experiencing it in ourselves and recog-
nizing it in each other."[19] Similarly, Alger would have read in Thomas Reid's *Essays* that "The man who acts according to the dictates
of his conscience, and takes due pains to be rightly informed of his
duty, is a perfect man with regard to morals, and merits no blame,
whatever may be the imperfections or errors of his understanding.
He who knowingly acts contrary to them is conscious of guilt, and
self-condemned. Every particular action that falls evidently within
the fundamental rules of morals is evidently his duty; and it requires
no reasoning to convince him that it is so."[20] That Alger himself
endorsed such doctrines of common-sense philosophy as these is
evident from his juvenile novels. The two fundamental assumptions
in his didactic fiction were that each of his young readers, like his
young heroes, was virtuous "by nature, but there is no one who
cannot be strengthened against temptation," and that each of them
should "do his duty as well and faithfully as he knew how, and trust
to Providence for the issue" (ETB, 166; SH, 52).
    To be sure, neither Alger nor the Harvard moral philosphers who

influenced him condemned those who won worldly wealth. Indeed, they praised the enlightened merchant-princes of State Street as harbingers of material prosperity and spiritual progress. However, the Unitarian moralists also taught that "the 'passion' for easy money"[21] was a curse, and Alger also learned this lesson well. For example, he later would frequently and explicitly caution his readers against idle speculation in the stock market, as in *Struggling Upward* (1886), in which he claimed that "Wall Street speculation" was a more corrupting influence on lives "than extravagant habits of living" (SU, 77). In short, as one of the moral elite educated at Harvard during this period, Alger was predisposed by heritage and intellectual training to emphasize in his fiction the efficacy of Christian morality, not the supposed benefits of crass materialism.

Alger concluded his brief autobiographical statement in the Class Book of 1852 with a paean to Harvard. "No period of my life," he wrote, "has been one of such unmixed happiness as the four years which have been spent within college walls. Whatever may be the course of my life hereafter, I shall never cease to regard it with mingled feeling of pleasure and regret—pleasure which the recollection of past happiness never fails to excite—regret that it is gone forever." His only other regret at the age of twenty, as he noted, was that he had not yet "known what it is to be looked up to as the teacher of a country school. I have not the satisfaction of knowing that some of the future orators, statesmen, and poets of America will become such through the profound impressions made upon them by my instructions."[22] Alger finally would realize his ambition to be a moral teacher of American youth, a hope molded in its turn by the instruction of the Harvard moral philosophers, when he became a writer of didactic juvenile stories over a dozen years later.

III   *Try and Trust*

The ensuing several years of Alger's life were marred by his indecisive search for a suitable career, and probably punctuated by recurrent personal frustrations. During the year following his graduation from Harvard, he lived in Marlborough with his parents and attempted, by both teaching and writing there, to remedy the deficiency mentioned in the Class Book as well as to support himself.[23] The attempt ended in failure. During this year, Alger worked on a "History of Middlesex County" and contributed poetry to magazines and newspapers,[24] but abandoned the unfinished history and entered Cambridge Divinity School in September, 1853. In November, 1853, he withdrew from the divinity school to assume duties as an assistant editor of the Boston *Daily Advertiser*, then owned and managed by members of the Hale family. Alger held this position until the following May. In June, 1854, he accepted the post of assistant teacher in Potowome Boarding School in East Greenwich, Rhode Island, where he remained nearly two years. He next became principal of the boys' academy in Deerfield, Massachusetts, during the summer term of 1856. The following year, until September, 1857, Alger again was employed as a private tutor in Boston and in addition served as a "joint editorial writer for the [Boston newspaper] *True Flag* with [John T.] Trowbridge."[25] Finally, he reentered the Cambridge Divinity School, and graduated in 1860.

Meanwhile, during these years of irregular employment, Alger inaugurated his professional writing career. He did not turn immediately to writing juvenile fiction, as those familiar with his reputation may assume, but tried originally to establish his credentials as a writer of sentimental-didactic fiction for adults. As Alger himself recalled in an essay written late in his career, "When I began to write for publication it was far from my expectation that I should devote my life to writing stories for boys. I was ambitious, rather, to write for adults."[26] Between 1852 and 1860, Alger published eleven original stories for adults in *Gleason's Pictorial Drawing Room Companion*, thirty-one in *Gleason's Weekly Line-of-Battle Ship*, thirteen in *The Flag of Our Union*, four in *True Flag*, one in *Ballou's Dollar Monthly*, and one story and a poem in *Peterson's Magazine*.[27] Many of these stories were reprinted in other magazines. Alger also wrote eight serials, some under the pseudonym Charles F. Preston, for the New York *Sun* and *Weekly Sun* newspapers, then edited by Moses Beach, during the late 1850s.[28] In addition, Alger published his first two books. A miscellaneous collection of his previously published poems and stories, *Bertha's Christmas Vision: An Autumn Sheaf*, was issued in 1856 by a Boston publisher, and his satirical poem of nearly four hundred lines, *Nothing to Do*, appeared anonymously the following year.[29] Alger also enjoyed limited success in contributing to three prestigious monthly magazines—*Putnam's*, *Graham's*, and *Harper's*. Although all editorial records of his contributions to the original *Putnam's* have been lost, he unquestionably wrote at least one poem and two stories which appeared in the issues of 1857, the final year of the magazine's original publication before its suspension during the financial crisis that year.[30] One of Alger's adult stories appeared in *Graham's*, and at least one of his stories and one of his poems appeared in *Harper's Monthly* during this period as well.[31]

The period that immediately followed Alger's graduation from Harvard probably was also marked by his introduction to Ralph Waldo Emerson. On December 28, 1853, the senior Alger, who by this time had become a member of the Marlborough town government, invited Emerson to lecture before the local Mechanics' Institute sometime during the early months of 1854.[32] Emerson undoubtedly accepted the invitation, because the younger Alger mentioned in a letter over forty years later that Emerson once had been "a guest at our house."[33]

Briefly, in the early 1860s, Alger threw over fiction to flirt, albeit only temporarily, with the travel essay, like didactic fiction a *genre* congenial to the men of genteel letters. He wrote at least one such essay for his hometown newspaper—"A Visit to the Falls of Montmorenci," which appeared in the Marlborough *Mirror* in May, 1860. The exercise could have been a rehearsal for those essays he wrote about his first journey to Europe later that year.[34] On September 5, 1860, after his graduation from Cambridge Divinity School, Alger, a cousin, and a classmate embarked for Europe and the *Wanderjahr* traditional among young men of their social class. After a hurried trip through Wales, Scotland, Ireland, and England, including a visit to Sir Walter Scott's home in Edinburgh, Alger and his companions spent the next several months touring the continent, visiting France, Belgium, Holland, the Rhine, southern Germany, Switzerland, and Italy, in the last country bearing diplomatic dispatches from Rome to Naples. While in Europe, Alger acted "as a foreign correspondent" and submitted a series of "European letters" to the New York *Sun* and occasional letters to the Boston *Transcript* and other publications.[35] While in Paris on February 22, 1861, Alger witnessed the funeral and burial of Eugene Scribe. Although he apparently did not purposefully attend the ceremonies, his observations later enabled him to write an essay on Scribe which appeared in the October, 1863, issue of the *North American Review.*[36]

Alger's life during the early years of the Civil War (1861–64) is very scantily documented. However, it can be established that in late April, 1861, soon after the firing on Fort Sumter, Alger returned to Massachusetts, first to Dover where he preached regularly from the Unitarian pulpit, then in December to Cambridge, where he again established himself as a private instructor.[37] He remained in Cambridge until 1864,[38] although he did teach at least one summer term in the Nahant, Massachusetts, schools, where one of his students was the young Robert Grant, later a distinguished literary figure.[39] In July, 1863, Alger was drafted into the militia, but he was exempted, probably for a physical disability.[40] That he vigorously supported the Union cause is certain, however. He corresponded regularly with one Joseph F. Dean, a young Massachusetts soldier whom he had befriended.[41] His earliest juvenile fiction, the three-volume "Campaign series," written during these war years, was designed to arouse sympathy for the war effort among its young readers. Alger also continued to write adult fiction, much of it with the same design. Although he was still unable to support himself with his pen alone, he was placing his adult fiction with reputable publishers more frequently. During the Civil War, two more of his stories appeared in *Harper's Monthly*, five appeared in *Frank Leslie's Illustrated Newspaper*, in some cases under the Preston pseudonym,[42] and he published "a large number of stories and poems" in *Harper's Weekly*.[43] His stories also continued to appear regularly in lesser magazines, and in addition he composed mediocre patriotic verse, most of which appeared in newspapers.[44]

Additional records which are available from this period 1861–1864 attest to the recurrence of the pattern already established in Alger's life: the well-educated recruit of the moral elite seeks a respectable niche in the cultured class. In March, 1862, for example, Alger was invited to occupy the pulpit of the Unitarian society in Alton, Illinois, but he declined, apparently because he did not wish to sever his connections with Eastern society and move to the West. He was made a member of the New England Genealogical Society in December, 1862, and the next year was elected an officer of that organization.[45] During his residence in Cambridge in these years, Alger may have joined the Examiners Club, a group of young Boston intellectuals whose membership included the Unitarian minister and author Edward Everett Hale, whom Alger probably first met in 1853–54 while employed by the Hale family-owned Boston *Daily Advertiser*.[46]

IV   *The Turn to Juvenile Fiction*

In 1864, Alger began the crucial transition from writing for adults to writing for juveniles, although the reason for the transition remains unclear. Alger himself offered two different, if related, reasons, and in any event he probably at first considered the juvenile literature he submitted to various magazines only a temporary expedient. For the public record, he claimed he did it in order to gain renown. As a writer of fiction for adults, he later claimed,

> I achieved fair success, but I could see that I had so many competitors that it would take a long time to acquire a reputation. One day I selected a plot for a two-column sketch for the Harpers. It was during the war. Thinking the matter over, it occurred to me that it would be a good plot for a juvenile book. I sat down at once and wrote to A. K. Loring, of Boston, at that time a publisher in only a small way, detailing the plot and asking if he would encourage me to write a juvenile book. He answered: "Go ahead, and if I don't publish it, some other publisher will." In three months I put in his hands the manuscript of "Frank's Campaign." This story was well received, but it was not till I removed to New York and wrote "Ragged Dick" that I scored a decided success.[47]

This sentimental account of his seemingly serendipitous success as a writer of boys' books, however, discounts a more realistic explanation for his decision to write for the juvenile market—that he did so from the necessity to earn a living. While turning out about two hundred stories for adults over slightly more than a decade, Alger still had to resort to a variety of teaching and editing jobs to supplement his income. Writing juvenile fiction offered him, at age thirty-two, a better opportunity to support himself by his pen. Alger admitted as much to E. C. Stedman, an eminent poet and critic, in a surprisingly candid response to a letter of congratulation upon the appearance of his volume of poetry in 1875. This letter merits lengthy quotation, for in it Alger offered a low estimation of his talent and his work, revealed a willingness to pander to those eminent writers whose achievements and reputations he envied, and explained that his decision to write juvenile literature was prompted entirely by mercenary motives:

> My dear Mr. Stedman,
>   Many thanks for the kind words with which you acknowledge the receipt of my little volume. I am afraid you do me too much honor in calling me

a fellow craftsman, but I am glad to accept the pleasant title. The *res angusta donis* of which Horace speaks compelled me years since to forsake the higher walks of literature, and devote myself to an humbler department which would pay me better. The decision was made when for an article in the North American Review on which I had expended considerable labor I was paid at the rate of a dollar per printed page. From that time I leased my pen to the boys, and the world has been spared much poor poetry and ambitious prose.[48]

A third, more innocuous account of Alger's transition to juvenile literature appeared in a biographical sketch of him in an 1885 issue of *Golden Argosy*: "At the request of a personal friend, he prepared a short sketch for *The Student and Schoolmate*. This was so widely copied and attracted so much favorable notice, that Mr. Alger saw that juvenile literature was his field. He straightway took possession and has occupied it ever since."[49]

V   Ministry in Brewster

The pressing need to earn his living may also account for Alger's decision, in November, 1864, finally to abandon Cambridge and to accept the invitation to settle over the First Unitarian Church and Society of Brewster, Massachusetts, at a salary of eight hundred dollars per year.[50] His departure from Cambridge was undoubtedly a difficult one, for twenty years later he reminisced with a young Cambridge correspondent that "Cambridge was for ten years my own residence, and I can say with truth that those ten years were among the happiest I have spent. Though I enjoy New York, I miss the literary atmosphere of that famous university town, and the special advantages which its residents command."[51] Still, he did leave Cambridge, and was installed in the Brewster parish on December 8, 1864. At Alger's invitation, Edward Everett Hale, who had become nationally famous by this time as the author of "The Man Without a Country," presided at the ordination.[52]

While in Brewster, Alger completed *Paul Prescott's Charge*, the second volume in his "Campaign series" for boys, and *Helen Ford*, a novel for mature girls and young women, both of which were published by Loring. In early 1866, moreover, Alger learned that Evert A. Duyckinck had selected him for inclusion in his newest edition of *The Cyclopedia of American Literature*.[53] However, Alger's ministry in Brewster, launched auspiciously enough by Hale and enhanced by the spread of his literary reputation, abruptly ended only fifteen months after it began. On March 19, 1866, a special committee comprised of three adult male church members who had been commissioned to investigate "certain reports in relation to Mr. Alger," reported to the parish standing committee, which in turn forwarded a letter to the secretary of the American Unitarian Association in Boston, excerpts from which follow:

> Horatio Alger, Jr. who has officiated as our Minister for about fifteen months past has recently been charged with gross immorality and a most heinous crime, a crime of no less magnitude than the abominable and revolting crime of unnatural familiarity with *boys*, which is too revolting to think of in the most brutal of our race— the commission of which under any circumstances, is to a refined or Christian mind too utterly incomprehensible— . . . .
>
> An able committee of the church and society . . . now verbally report, that on the examination of two boys (and they have good reason to think there are others) they were entirely confirmed and unanimous in the opinion of his being guilty to the full extent of the above specified charges.
>
> Whereupon the committee sent for Alger and to him specified the charges and evidence of his guilt, which he neither denied or attempted to extenuate but received with the apparent calmness of an old offender—and hastily left town on the next train for parts unknown—probably Boston.
>
> Had he remained longer an arrest or something worse might have occurred. We should scarcely have felt responsible for the consequences in an outraged community, and that outrage committed by a pretended Christian teacher.
>
> No further comment is necessary. You know the penalty attached to such unnatural crime by human as well as divine bars. Please take such action as will prevent his imposing on others and advise us as to what further duties devolve on us as a Christian Society.

On his part, according to the special investigating committee of the church, Alger "admitted that he had been imprudent" and considered his connection with the society dissolved.[54] Disgraced and humiliated, throughout the remainder of his life he attempted to conceal the fact that he had preached in Brewster and that his connection with the Unitarian society there had been dissolved because he had been accused of homosexual acts with boys in his congregation. In early 1869, for example, Alger asked a correspondent to "be kind enough in addressing me to omit the 'Rev.' as I wish my name identified only with the literary profession."[55] The best two biographical sketches of Alger that appeared during his life and for which he was interviewed—the first published in *Golden Argosy* in 1885 and the second in *Munsey's Magazine* in 1892—fail to mention Brewster at all. As late as 1896, in reply to a friend's query, Alger contended that "I studied theology chiefly as a branch of literary culture and without any intention of devoting myself to it as a profession."[56] Alger's ardent desire to maintain an unblemished reputation during these years informs a reading of several of his juvenile novels. Through the creaky plot machinations in *Paul the Peddler* (1871), for example, Alger contrasted the disreputable rogues who assume a variety of aliases and the reputable hero who is cleared of false allegations by the testimony of a friend.

VI   *Adrift in the City*

Though certainly disgraced, Alger's more immediate problem in the spring of 1866 was his loss of regular employment. Rather than secluding himself in Boston as his prosecutors suspected, he avoided that reproving sanctuary of orthodoxy, social propriety, family, and old friends, and instead surfaced in New York a month after his departure from Brewster, claiming, as he wrote to William Conant Church, the editor of *The Galaxy*, that "I have established myself in New York with the intention of devoting myself solely to literary pursuits and increasing my acquaintances with publishers."[57]

Alger's "literary pursuits" in New York inclined him even more strongly toward the writing of didactic fiction for boys, and his reasons for doing so require some elaboration. Although he came to a city where his past would remain shrouded in obscurity, Alger did not escape reproach, for it seems that he was his own chief accuser. A poem, "Friar Anselmo's Sin," which he submitted to Church under his covering letter only a few days after his disgrace before the Brewster parish committee, suggests that during this brief period Alger contemplated suicide, then resolved to expiate his "sin."[58] The poem begins

> Friar Anselmo (God's grace may he win!)
> Committed one sad day a deadly sin;
>
> Which being done he drew back, self-abhorred,
> From the rebuking presence of the Lord,
>
> And, kneeling down, besought, with bitter cry,
> Since life was worthless grown, that he might die.

Suddenly, however, a "cry of sharp distress" arouses Anselmo from his death-reverie, and he beholds "a wounded traveller" who has "crawled for aid unto the convent door." Like the Good Samaritan, Anselmo with "tender foresight cared for all his needs,—/A blessed ministry of noble deeds." After the traveler has recuperated and resumed his journey, Anselmo is visited by an angel who resembles "the poor wayfarer" and who counsels him to take

> "Courage, Anselmo, though thy sin be great,
> God grants thee life that thou may'st expiate.
>
> "Thy guilty stains shall be washed white again,
> By noble service done thy fellow-men.
>
> "His soul draws nearest unto God above,
> Who to his brother ministers in love."

Anselmo, his "soul lighted of its past despair," thereafter strives, "obeying God's high will,/His heaven-appointed mission to fulfil."

Alger, by defining the act of writing moral-didactic fiction *per se* as an act of charity, adopted Friar Anselmo's "ministry of noble deeds" as his own. As a Harvard-educated Unitarian and Massachusetts patrician, he apparently chose to atone for his "imprudence" by writing moralistic, didactic fiction for boys which endorsed environmental reforms. As Daniel W. Howe has concluded, the Harvard moralists believed that "the artist shared the hortatory function of the evangelical preacher: both were dedicated to emotional appeals on behalf of religion and morality."[59] Alger merely transferred his ministry from pulpit to pen. Indeed, in choosing to write didactic fiction designed to influence impressionable young readers to love "moral beauty" and to do good, Alger followed the example set by Andrews Norton, Joseph Tuckerman, William

Ellery Channing, and Henry Ware, Jr., earlier Unitarian ministers who composed didactic fiction or poetry.[60] As a patrician who had not yet settled upon his "calling," Alger after leaving Brewster wrote new juvenile novels about poor-but-virtuous heroes who, like Alger himself, aspire to rise to respectability; and he populated these novels, unlike his earlier juvenile books, with Alger-like benevolent patrons who also have adopted Anselmo's "ministry of noble deeds." In short, Alger's two paramount problems in the spring of 1866— expiation and employment—had a single, practical solution. Not surprisingly, thirty years later he would write, "It seems to me that no writer should undertake to write for boys who does not feel that he has been called to that particular work."[61]

CHAPTER 2

"I Leased My Pen to the Boys"

I Street Life in New York

AT the age of thirty-five, Alger earnestly set about his self-ap-pointed task of sharing his moral vision with others, especially boys. Like most other moral reformers of his age, throughout his life he abstained from and discouraged others from the use of liquor and tobacco;[1] indeed, he had been elected president of the Cadets for Temperance in Brewster shortly before his enforced departure.[2] Soon after settling in New York, moreover, he became interested in the plight of the thousands of poor orphans and runaways who had been attracted to the city during and immediately after the Civil War. In the summer of 1866, for example, Alger attended a children's church service at the Five Points mission which, quite incidentally, led him to compose the ballad of "John Maynard," a popular declamation piece for schoolchildren in the late nineteenth century.[3] As his biographical sketch in *Golden Argosy* indicates, Alger "became a familiar figure along the docks, and wherever the friendless urchins could be found. His pleasant ways, his open-handed charity, and his thorough sympathy with the unfortunates rendered him a favorite wherever he went. One of his protegés once said to the writer that Mr. Alger could raise a regiment of boys in New York alone, who would fight to the death for him."[4]

A corresponding shift in the tone of Alger's fiction likewise oc-curred at this time. After arriving in New York, he briefly continued to mine the same sentimental vein that he had earlier found prof-itable. Compelled by circumstances to earn money as easily as pos-sible, he revised one of his old New York *Sun* serials to enhance its appeal to a juvenile audience, and Loring published it under the title *Charlie Codman's Cruise,* the third and final volume in his "Campaign series." He revised another of his earlier *Sun* serials, and Loring published it anonymously as *Timothy Crump's Ward,* an adult novel which sold poorly. After a five-year hiatus he again

33

submitted material to *Gleason's Literary Companion,* and he increasingly exploited the good offices of William T. Adams ("Oliver Optic"), editor of *The Student and Schoolmate,* to place his juvenile stories in that periodical. In the autumn of 1866, one of his stories also appeared in *Our Young Folks,* a Ticknor and Fields periodical designed to be an *Atlantic Monthly* for boys and girls, under the editorship of Alger's former editorial colleague J. T. Trowbridge. Alger continued to the end of his life to correspond with Trowbridge, who eventually gained considerable renown as a genteel man of letters.[5]

In early 1867, however, Alger finally struck the mother lode. Seemingly by accident, much as he fortuitously had stumbled upon Scribe's funeral procession in Paris years before, Alger wrote his first juvenile story about the young "street Arabs" of New York. Entitled "Ragged Dick; or, Street Life in New York," the brief serial began in the January, 1867, issue of *The Student and Schoolmate.* The serial was so favorably received that Alger rewrote and enlarged it, publishing it, according to his preface, as the first volume of a "series intended to illustrate the life and experiences of the friendless and vagrant children who are now numbered by thousands in New York and other cities." Alger indicated that the "necessary information has been gathered mainly from personal observation and conversations with the boys themselves" and the Superintendent of the Newsboys' Lodging House, a philanthropic institution sponsored by urban reformer Charles Loring Brace's Children's Aid Society. The preface to the book-length *Ragged Dick,* Alger's only best seller during his long writing career, concludes on a note especially significant in light of the undeserved reputation the author eventually acquired as a success-apologist: "The author hopes that, while the volumes in this series may prove interesting as stories, they may also have the effect of enlisting the sympathies of his readers in behalf of the unfortunate children whose life is described, and of leading them to co-operate with the praiseworthy efforts now making by the Children's Aid Society and other organizations to ameliorate their condition."[6] In short, Alger clearly intended *Ragged Dick* to evoke public sympathy for the urchin class upon whom his characters were modeled, not to arouse envy for them among his readers. The ragged hero of this story, encouraged to aspire to a respectable station in life by the staff of the Lodging House and other adults, through the peculiar principles of "luck and pluck" which animate Alger's fictional world realizes his ambition by novel's end—he acquires a new name, Richard Hunter, Esq., and a job as a clerk in a counting room at the munificent salary of ten dollars per week.

The successful serialization of "Ragged Dick" won for Alger a contract from his Boston publisher, A. K. Loring, for a total of six volumes in the same vein. "Great expectations were entertained respecting these books, and they were more than fulfilled. Their popularity was astonishing. Hundreds of Sunday-school libraries bought them, and they were read in every State and Territory in the Union."[7]

In his introduction to each of the five succeeding volumes in the "Ragged Dick series," Alger restated his essentially didactic purpose, and in his preface to the final volume in the series, *Rufus and Rose* (1870), he dutifully claimed that "invention has played but a subordinate part" in his depiction of the young vagabonds and their abject condition; then he stated explicitly that "the principal object" of the series has been to show that the large class of street boys— numbering thousands in New York alone—furnishes material out of which good citizens may be made, if the right influences are brought to bear upon them. In every case, therefore, the author has led his hero, step by step, from vagabondange to a position of respectability." In this preface Alger also announced that the program of environmental reform which he endorsed already had begun to pay dividends: an official of the Children's Aid Society had discovered in one Western town that a former street boy aided by the Society had become the district attorney, another a clergyman, still others "prosperous and even wealthy businessmen" (Ru&R, vii-viii). In other words, even early in his juvenile writing career, Alger, true to his Harvard training, scrupulously avoided offering only the businessman as an acceptable role-model of respectability to his young readers. And to insure that his moral message would be propagated, he advertised in his preface to *Fame and Fortune* (1868) that Loring would send free copies of volumes in the series "to any regularly organized Newsboys' Lodge within the United States."[8]

Despite the sales success of the early volumes in the "Ragged Dick series," Alger remained financially insecure. Apparently his generosity toward others increased in proportion to the increase in his income, for soon after settling in New York, certainly no later than 1869, he was again teaching private students in addition to

writing moral tales.[9] For a period of twelve years, beginning probably in 1869, Alger was charged with tutoring the five sons of Joseph
Seligman, the founder of an international banking firm.[10] Among
these sons were Isaac Newton Seligman (1855–1917), who in 1894
succeeded his father and uncle as head of the banking house J. &
W. Seligman and Company, and Edwin Robert Anderson Seligman
(1861–1939), who in 1904 became McVickar Professor of Political
Economy at Columbia University and, in 1902–03, served as president of the American Economic Association, which he had helped
organize in 1885.

Alger also assumed a variety of writing tasks to supplement his
income. Apparently through the intercession of Joseph Seligman,
who was a founder of the Hebrew Benevolent and Orphan Asylum
and a long-time member of the Board of Education in New York
City, Alger began contributing serials to the juvenile magazine
Young Israel in 1870. In addition, Alger continued to write sentimental adult fiction for *Gleason's Literary Companion* for a few
years after his arrival in New York; one of his novelle, "Ralph Raymond's Heir" (1869), written under the pseudonym Arthur Hamilton, was converted into a juvenile novel and published under
Alger's own name in 1892. And by the spring of 1870 at the latest,
Alger had begun collaborating with his cousin, a noted Unitarian
minister, on the two-volume *Life of Edwin Forrest*, a project sub-
sidized by the actor Forrest and his heirs.[11]

Meanwhile, though residing in New York, Alger carefully nur-
tured his past patrician associations with Harvard and Boston. In
the late 1860s and early 1870s, for example, he was an active member of the Harvard Club of New York. He attended several of its
annual dinners at Delmonico's, and indeed during these years he
sometimes composed the ode sung on the occasion. In 1869, as the
New York Times reported, those attending the dinner, including
William Cullen Bryant, Joseph H. Choate, and Charles Dana, sang
"the college ode, composed by HORATIO ALGER, of Boston."[12]
(Although a New York resident for nearly three years by this time,
Alger apparently reclaimed Boston residency on such special occasions as these.) In addition, he usually passed part of each summer
with his parents in South Natick, Massachusetts, and in January,
1874, was elected to membership in the local Historical Society
there.[13] Moreover, in late 1874, Alger's cousin, William Rounseville
Alger, a graduate of the Cambridge Theological School in 1847,

former minister of the liberal Bulfinch Street Society of Boston, and former chaplain of the Massachusetts House of Representatives,[14] was called to the pulpit of the Church of the Messiah in New York. His cousin was among the first new members enrolled in the church after his appointment, and until William left New York in 1878 the two men frequently fraternized.[15] Occasionally Alger also visited with friends from his Harvard years, as he did in 1875 with Joseph H. Choate.[16]

A reputable author and member of the Harvard Club, Alger throughout the remainder of his life exercised a certain discretion in discussing his probable homosexuality. Indeed, he mentioned such a sensitive subject on only one known occasion after his dismissal from the Brewster pulpit. In the spring of 1870, the elder Henry James wrote to Henry James, Jr., that Horatio Alger "talks freely about his own late insanity—which he in fact appears to enjoy as a subject of conversation and in which I believe he has somewhat interested William [James]."[17] Despite Alger's apparent willingness to discuss his "insanity," probably a polite reference to his sexual "aberration," with a professional physician and psychologist, the subject remained a carefully guarded, confidential one. Still, Alger occasionally did make cryptic reference to homosexuality in his juvenile fiction. These references suggest that Alger may have been insecure with his sexual orientation. The hero of his novel *Tattered Tom* (1871), for example, is actually female, despite her name. As if referring to himself, Alger noted that "it was not quite easy to determine whether it was a boy or girl" (TT, 10). In addition, one of Alger's stock characters in his juvenile novels is the "effeminate-looking young man, foppishly dressed" who invariably is the object of other characters' scorn and pity. One such character, named Percy de Brabazon, even speaks with a pronounced lisp (i.e., " 'He's the second cousin of a lord, and yet—you'll hardly cwedit it—we're weally vewy intimate' ") as Alger sought to endow him with the characteristics of a stereotyped homosexual (ANY, 14–15). In *Silas Snobden's Office Boy* (1889), moreover, a kidnapped boy is disguised as a girl and threatened with incarceration in an "insane asylum" (just as Alger himself may have been treated for his "aberration")[18] if he admits to anyone that he is a boy (SSOB, 217). Alger's wish to atone for the "secret sin" in his past may have spurred him to identify his own charitable acts of writing didactic books for boys with the acts of the charitable patrons in his books who wish to atone for a secret sin in their past by aiding the heroes. The patron in *Try and Trust* (1871), for example, conceals "some sad secret about which the world knew nothing" and rejoins the electric chain of humanity only after saving the hero's life (T&T, 81).

II *The Middle Years: The 1870s*

Although Alger sought little personal publicity during most of his life, he was active in publicizing environmental reforms and his own commitment to them. His most noteworthy crusade for one such reform, children's aid, occurred in 1872. Early in that year, Alger contacted A. E. Cerqua, superintendent of the Italian school at the Five Points in New York, and G. F. Secchi de Casale, editor of the ethnic newspaper *Eco d'Italia,* to obtain information about the infamous padrone system, which allowed an overseer to lease young Italian boys from their parents, ship them to America, teach them rudimentary musical skills, and profit from their beggary on the streets of many American cities.[19] Alger intended the work that resulted from his investigation, *Phil the Fiddler* (1872), to be a humanitarian exposé of the corrupt scheme; as he wrote in his preface to this book, "If the story of 'Phil, the Fiddler,' in revealing for the first time to the American public the hardships and ill-treatment of these wandering musicians, shall excite an active sympathy in their behalf, the author will feel abundantly repaid for his labors" (PF, 282). The importance of Alger's book to the campaign against the padrone system, a campaign that culminated in the enactment by the New York state legislature in 1874 of a child abuse law, was probably slight, inasmuch as no contemporary authority corroborates the claim;—which probably originated with Alger himself;—that "Within six months from the appearance of the book, the leading newspapers of New York, having vigorously co-operated in exposing the cruelties practiced by the padrones, the system was effectually broken up, not only in New York but in all the large cities of America."[20] Still, whether or not the book was instrumental in that effort, Alger apparently believed that it had been crucial and that his moral purpose had been well served. The patrician attitude toward social reform which is evident in *Phil* also informs a reading of *Julius, or The Street Boy Out West* (1874), another volume in the "Tattered Tom series." In the preface to this book about a "street

Arab" who finds a home in a small Western town, Alger acknowledged his indebtedness for the characters and plot to Charles Loring Brace's *The Dangerous Classes of New York* and the program of orphan resettlement administered by the Children's Aid Society (Jul, ix).

In the summer of 1873 Alger embarked on a second grand tour of Europe, on this occasion accompanied at his invitation by three members of his immediate family, including his parents. Although few details are available, references to the trip in Alger's work and elsewhere establish that the party visited England, including Stratford-on-Avon and Sir Walter Scott's home in Abbotsford, Switzerland, Austria, including the Vienna Exposition, and Italy, including Florence, Verona, and Venice.[21]

Although Alger once claimed that after he began to write juvenile fiction he "soon found reason to believe that I was much more likely to achieve success as a writer for boys than as a writer for adults . . . [and] therefore confined myself to juvenile fiction,"[22] the record reveals that he did not renounce his ambition to write respectable adult works. For example, the adult novella *Ralph Raymond's Heir* was written after he supposedly had confined himself exclusively to the juvenile market. Between 1872 and 1878, over two dozen of Alger's adult stories originally published during the 1850s and 1860s were reprinted in *Gleason's Monthly Companion.* In addition, between 1875 and 1878, Alger wrote several works for adults in an apparent attempt to broaden his audience and enhance his reputation as a man of letters. In 1875, Loring issued *Grand'ther Baldwin's Thanksgiving,* a volume of Alger's poetry composed over the preceding twenty years. In general, the book was favorably reviewed,[23] and its author received "letters of appreciation from Longfellow, Stedman,[24] Professor William Mathews [later of the University of Chicago and a minor author in his own right], B. P. Shillaber ["Mrs. Partington"], and others."[25] Encouraged by this response, Alger wrote an adult novella in 1877, anonymously published by Loring, entitled *The New Schoolma'am; or, A Summer in North Sparta.* "If successful," he wrote to his former pupil E. R. A. Seligman, "I shall probably write one novel a year."[26] About five months later Alger elatedly quoted from a favorable review of his novella which had appeared in the London *Academy* in another letter to Seligman, and, in July, 1878, he wrote again to explain that he had completed yet another new novel for adults, although his publisher was postponing its appearance until the book trade improved.[27] The original manuscript of this work, "Mabel Parker; or, The Hidden Treasure," remains unpublished.

III   A Celebrated Traveler

Especially during the late 1870s, Alger turned his penchant for travel to double advantage. His travels enabled him to inject local color and realistic detail into his fiction, and also gave him the opportunity to enjoy his small measure of fame and to be received as an eminent man of culture and education. After the sales success of his "Ragged Dick series," according to the best available evidence, Alger's sales stagnated. His "Tattered Tom series" of eight books (1871–79), "Luck and Pluck series" of eight books (1869–75), and "Brave and Bold series" of four books (1872–77) simply failed to sell as well as his earliest juvenile books. Consequently, he traveled to the West Coast via transcontinental railroad in 1877 and to Colorado in 1878 to gather material for a new series of four local-color juveniles, the "Pacific series", which he hoped would stimulate declining reader interest in his work.[28] Although the books that resulted from these trips exploited a more sensational vein than had his earlier juvenile books, they failed to stem the decline in his popularity.

Still, Alger was able to act the role of venerable social lion while traveling. On his way to the Pacific coast in the early spring of 1877, he spent several days in Omaha with the family of U.S. Senator Phineas W. Hitchcock of Nebraska, and he was escorted around Salt Lake City by a leading businessman in the town, one of the original Mormon immigrants to the West.[29] In San Francisco, he was introduced to historian H. H. Bancroft and businessmen Ignatz and Jesse Seligman.[30] After traveling through Southern California and before returning to the East, Alger toured the Pacific Northwest, where he visited wealthy friends.[31] Interviewed by the editor of the Portland *Oregonian,* he was described in that newspaper as "a cultivated and affable gentleman."[32] The next spring Alger left New York for Denver, stopping en route "at Philadelphia, Washington, Cincinnati, & St. Louis" as well as Topeka, Kansas, and Pueblo, Colorado. Except in Topeka, as he wrote to Seligman, "I had friends who made my stay pleasant. At Cincinnati, I dined with the editor of the Daily Gazette, at St. Louis I attended a little party besides spending another evening out."[33] In October, 1887, Alger went to Chicago to obtain material for his juvenile novel *Luke Walton, or The Chicago Newsboy* (1887–88),[34] and during the autumn of 1890 he traveled to the West Coast via Northern Pacific railroad for a similar reason.[35] As late as 1896 he was contemplating yet another trip to California.[36] During the last two decades of his life Alger frequented the exclusive Eastern resort towns of Saratoga, Hampton Beach, Martha's Vineyard, and Old Orchard Beach, Maine,[37] and allusions to these summer resorts occasionally appeared in his work. At least once, in 1879, the Seligman family entertained him at their summer home in Long Branch, New Jersey.[38]

Alger's reputation as a gentleman and his intimacy with the Seligman family were undoubtedly two factors that led to his appointment as tutor to his most famous private pupil—Benjamin Cardozo, who served as an Associate Justice of the U.S. Supreme Court from 1932 until 1938. The Cardozo and Seligman families were near neighbors in Long Branch, and Alger may have first met young Cardozo during a visit there. At any rate, during the late 1870s and early 1880s the penny-watching Alger continued to tutor students privately, apparently because his attempt to inject local color into his Western juvenile books had failed to bolster his sagging sales and income. (In a letter to Seligman in the autumn of 1879 he complained about the slow book trade of the preceding two years, during which time he had published the four volumes of his "Pacific series," and indicated that he hoped "to spend a couple of hours daily in teaching during the coming year.")[39] In 1883, when young Cardozo began his private study preparatory to admission to Columbia University for the fall term of 1885, Alger was hired as his tutor. Years later, when asked about his college preparation, Justice Cardozo acknowledged that Alger had been charged with that responsibility and added that "he did not do as successful a job for me as he did with the careers of his newsboy heroes."[40]

IV   *Political Animadversions*

Alger's political views, which he increasingly expressed during the late 1870s and 1880s, were those of "Unitarian Whiggery," as Daniel Howe has described the politics of the Harvard moral elite. During the second term of his senior year at Harvard, Alger had

satisfied a course requirement in Political Economy.[41] Although
Francis Bowen's textbook *Political Economy* was not published until
1856 and hence not yet available to Alger as a Harvard student, the
principles of Unitarian Whiggery which Bowen articulated had been
well established long before that time and formed the cornerstone
of the course. Bowen, like Alger, was suspicious of the dogma and
abstract logic of classical economic theorizing, and preferred to conceive of society as an organic whole with interrelated parts rather
than as a series of market transactions. The major defect of abstract,
classical economics, Bowen averred, was its tendency to generalize
economic principles whose applicability was limited to specific times
and places. "If Adam Smith were living in our own day," he once
wrote, "it may be doubted whether he would be the uncompro-
mising advocate that he was of Free Trade."[42] Similarly, Alger, with
his fond memories of antebellum Marlborough and its preindustrial
economy, was not blind to the human suffering infecting, in stark
contrast, the modern industrial city. Consequently, his commitment
to classical economics was not absolute. To be sure, from one side
of his mouth he vigorously defended property rights and economic
orthodoxy, but from the other side he could speculate on the prac-
ticality of economic cooperation. Especially in his fiction, he both
embraced the doctrines of the "fair price" and the "just wage" and
condemned the power of concentrated wealth to interfere with
market forces.

Alger frequently expressed interest in the principle of economic
cooperation. As early as 1872, after a fire devastated several of the
warehouses of the Boston publishers Lee and Shepard, Alger wrote
to offer his sympathy even though he had no professional association
with them. He explained that "In these days authors and publishers
are mutually interested in each other's welfare and prosperity.
There is not that natural antagonism which was once supposed to
exist."[43] In 1877 he enthusiastically noted in a letter to Seligman
that he had visited the Zion Cooperative Store in Salt Lake City,[44]
and about eight years later, after Seligman had been appointed a
political economist at Columbia and begun his lifelong research into
the merits of socialism, his former tutor mailed to him "a condensed
statement of the operations of the cooperative store in Natick. You
will see [Alger opined] that it has been a remarkable success, and
paid extraordinary dividends. Yet I do not know that there has been
anything exceptionally favorable in the circumstances attending its

formation and history. The secret of its success has been good management, and where cooperation fails, I suspect that failure is due to poor management."[45] In short, as a student of the anti-Darwinian naturalist Louis Agassiz,[46] Alger refused to adopt even for rhetorical purposes Herbert Spencer's and Charles Darwin's ideas of natural selection and the survival of the fittest to justify corporate activities during the Gilded Age. Never a social Darwinist, he doubted the efficacy of ruthless economic competition. In *Paul the Peddler* (1871), for example, he explicitly criticized intense economic competition as both inefficient and dehumanizing.

Alger also frequently expressed in his fiction his anachronistic economic opinions about wages, prices, and entrenched capital. Although these opinions are considered more fully in a subsequent chapter, each one may be briefly outlined here. Like Joseph Tuckerman, his father's predecessor in Chelsea, and his own student E. R. A. Seligman, Alger endorsed the doctrine of the "just" or "living wage." As Daniel W. Howe explains, this medieval Christian notion was defended by the Unitarian moralists, in particular Tuckerman, even though they also subscribed to the more orthodox and modern commodity theory of wages. The hero of Alger's novel *Five Hundred Dollars* (1888–89), for example, complains that the owner of an unmechanized shoe factory (modeled after the shoe factory Alger knew as a boy in Marlborough) "pays low wages all around" and that most of his employees could not afford to move their families to find more lucrative employment ($500, 50). Alger also recommended that merchants establish "fair prices" for all customers in lieu of charging what the market will bear and accumulating a large profit, for, as he insisted in *Mark the Match Boy* (1869), "fair prices in the long run are the best for all parties" (MMB, 290). Also in his fiction Alger warned against the power of concentrated wealth. He frequently depicted the plight of a poor, dependent seamstress who toils long hours for the few cents per day paid her by an impersonal store, and who constantly fears that she will lose even this paltry income if she only once fails to please the store owners. One such character, the mother of the young hero in *Luke Walton* (1887–88), concludes that "Money makes people mean and unjust" (LW, 135).

Alger's political conservatism is evident in his letters and in a series of three juvenile biographies of "illustrious Americans." The letters reveal that he proudly voted for Rutherford Hayes in 1876 and contemplated with dismay Samuel Tilden's victory in that Presidential race.[47] He also supported William Henry Harrison in 1888, anti-Tammany candidates in New York, and the William McKinley-Theodore Roosevelt national candidacies in 1896, reserving his strongest political endorsement for a distant relative, Civil War General Russell A. Alger, a former governor of Michigan who was once considered a leading candidate for President.[48] Alger's monetary orthodoxy seems evident from his critique of William Jennings Bryan and "free silver" during the 1896 campaign; he believed the Gold Democrats offered a "good ticket."[49] His first juvenile biography, about Whig Senator Daniel Webster, appeared in 1870 and was reissued in 1883; his other two biographies, of Republican Presidents Garfield and Lincoln, were published in 1881 and 1882, respectively. These fictionalized biographies of political leaders can be distinguished from Alger's juvenile novels only on the basis of the hero's reward—a fact that in turn suggests how easily Alger could assimilate political conservatism into his peculiarly moral vision.

V   Late Years and Retirement

During the years immediately preceding his retirement in 1896, Alger ground out dozens of juvenile novels with only slight regard for their literary quality. Francis S. Street, co-publisher of a sensational newspaper, the New York Weekly, and Frank Munsey, the ambitious publisher of Golden Argosy, began serializing Alger's stories in 1871 and 1882, respectively,[50] and Alger increasingly diluted his works to satisfy the increased demands for wordspace. His contributions to Golden Argosy during its heyday became so frequent, in fact, that the pen name "Arthur Lee Putnam" was invented for his use in those serializations that overlapped with others bearing Alger's own name; but when issued as single volumes, these works appear with Alger's name alone as author. The bankrupted Loring had retired from publishing in 1881 after issuing most of Alger's disappointing "Pacific series"; thereafter, the Philadelphia publisher Henry T. Coates became Alger's primary book distributor, and his firm issued, inexorably, Alger's four-volume "Atlantic series" (1883–86), his four-volume "Way to Success series" (1887–90), and his three-volume "New World series" (1892–93). In most of his books during the 1880s and 1890s, however, Alger abandoned all pretense of writing installments in a thematically united series. Instead, like many another formula writer, he played very slight, safe variations on the same timeworn theme. Alger acknowledged that all of his juvenile novels bore this "family resemblance," but he claimed that because his young readers did not seem to object, neither should the adult reviewers.[51]

Although the always questionable quality of his fiction deteriorated during the 1880s and 1890s, Alger maintained a steady interest in such manifestations of high culture as Harvard University, professional theater, and genteel letters. For example, he approvingly mentioned in correspondence that his cousin, Frank Cushman "of Mayflower memory," as well as the son of General Russell Alger, attended Harvard, his alma mater.[52] Moreover, Alger continued to attend Harvard Club functions, including its 1892 annual dinner, and the fortieth reunion of his class in 1892.[53] He befriended a member of Joseph Jefferson's theatrical company;[54] frequently attended New York and Boston stage productions, such as *Sue,* a play by Bret Harte;[55] and watched Mark Twain perform on stage on at least three occasions.[56] He continued to read avidly the *Atlantic Monthly,* the *North American Review,* and the novels of Howells, alluding to him in his juvenile fiction as the preeminent American novelist of the day.[57] In 1895 he wrote to Albert Bigelow Paine to promise to "take the opportunity some day to call at your office."[58] He freely alluded to the works of such writers as Alexander Pope, Oliver Wendell Holmes, and William Cullen Bryant in his letters.[59] Indeed, the New England Brahmin poets Henry Wadsworth Longfellow, James Russell Lowell, and Holmes remained among his favorite authors. When Longfellow died in 1882, he wrote a brief poem to commemorate the passing of his old teacher.[60] Alger once described Lowell, his father's classmate in the Harvard class of 1825, as the possessor of "high poetical and critical gifts," and occasionally mentioned his work in his juvenile books.[61] Alger paid Holmes the compliment, albeit a dubious one, of modeling his final novel for adults, *The Disagreeable Woman: A Social Mystery* (1895), published under the pseudonym "Julian Starr," upon Holmes's Breakfast Table books.[62] Clamoring after his own small measure of genteel respectability, Alger welcomed any small suggestion that he was popular among serious readers, such as the news of his election to honorary membership in the Chester Literary Union of New York, the notification in 1894 that his books were recommended reading in a class at Drake University, and the news that his anonymously published adult novel *Timothy Crump's Ward* had been one of the most widely circulated volumes in the Boston Public Library during one year.[63]

A Massachusetts patrician to his death, Alger also maintained his personal interest in reform. Motivated by the same moral purpose that spurred him to write didactic juvenile fiction, he publicly addressed audiences of young boys and at least once spoke before the Women's Suffrage League of Boston, often reading excerpts from *Ragged Dick* to such groups.[64] In addition, he informally adopted three boys—much as one of his benevolent patrons might have done—during the 1880s and early 1890s. The first young man Alger provided with a small business in Biddeford, Maine.[65] The second, a fifteen-year-old orphan whom he adopted in 1884, was sent to a commercial school at eighteen, was apprenticed to a photographer at nineteen, and in 1895 "passed the civil service examination and became one of Theodore Roosevelt's reform police."[66] The youngest adopted boy, aged fourteen when Alger assumed charge of him in early 1894 and the brother of Alger's second adopted son, was sent in 1898, at age eighteen, to the same commercial school to receive a business education. "I may not be able to leave Tommy much," Alger wrote that year, "but I mean to leave him a better education at any rate."[67] After his self-described nervous "breakdown" in 1896, Alger regretted the need to restrict his charitable activities. In a barely legible scrawl, he wrote to Russell A. Alger in 1898 that "With such means as I had I have been able to do a good deal of charitable work, but I doubt if I shall be able to very much more."[68]

Acquiring the means to do his charitable work—to patronize his young friends and adopted sons—became increasingly difficult for Alger in the 1890s. Although he was conscious of the steady deterioration in the quality of his fiction, he found such hack writing necessary to earn his living. In his letters he often admitted that he considered writing a burden and frequently expressed concern about the size of his royalty checks. His books did not sell well during this decade at least partly because, as Alger himself conceded, they did not merit large sales. For example, he noted in 1895 that "I hardly thought [*The Disagreeable Woman*] worth" its elaborate binding.[69] A year later, he admitted that he "didn't care much" for *Adrift in the City*, his latest juvenile novel.[70] In the summer of 1896, overworked and undercompensated, he broke down completely, and retired to his sister's home in South Natick to await death.

Accustomed to a minimum payment of a mere two hundred and fifty dollars for a complete serial plus royalties from book sales, Alger once estimated his total income from writing during his residence in New York betwen 1866 and 1896 at only a hundred thousand dollars.[71] His income was so reduced by late 1898 that he arranged for Edward Stratemeyer, an editorial friend who later became a notable juvenile author in his own right, to complete sub rosa his half-finished manuscript of *Out for Business.*[72] While negotiating with Stratemeyer, Alger expressed concern whether "it were really worth fixing up—*It is a good deal below my average,* having been written when I was in a state of nervous depression." Worried by his reduced income, he wrote to Stratemeyer that his "kinsman Secretary Alger . . . is reputed to be worth ten millions." Half-seriously, he mocked, "Why, oh why didn't I go into the war business?"[73]

The news of Alger's death on July 18, 1899, warranted only brief notice in major newspapers, when mentioned at all. His news service obituary, written from the 1875 edition of Duyckinck's *Cyclopedia of American Literature,* was a compendium of misinformation.[74] Although Alger was not destitute at his death—he became a silent partner in a Boston business in 1897 so that he would be less dependent on the declining income from his writing,[75] and he owned property in North Chicago—he was hardly prosperous. In his will he bequeathed less than a thousand dollars in cash to friends and relatives; instead, copyrights, manuscripts, and his private library comprised most of his bequests.[76] Alger's old friend Frank Munsey published one of the few posthumous tributes to him, but it did not appear until nearly a decade after Alger's death, and then in a privately printed volume. Munsey wrote that "he was one of the most human men I have ever known—a man with the simplicity of a child and the sweet, pure soul of God's best type of woman. He left behind him many books, which delighted the youth of our land, and which still delight the boys and girls of the present generation. My own interest in *The Argosy* was scarcely more than Mr. Alger's, and from the first issue of the publication to the end of his life he gave it the best work of his pen."[77] After the turn of the century this sentimental, distorted view of Alger's character became the rule rather than the exception, its significance magnified by the swell in the sales of his once unpopular books.

CHAPTER 3

The Adult Fiction

ALTHOUGH Horatio Alger's fame rests upon the prodigious production of over a hundred juvenile novels written between 1864 and his death in 1899, he also had a career as a writer of adult fiction, most of which is now generally ignored. Alger published twelve adult novelle between 1857 and 1869; by that time the demand for his juvenile work had increased substantially, following the publication in 1868 of his best seller for boys, *Ragged Dick; or, Street Life in New York,* and he then turned his attention to writing fiction almost exclusively for this market. In addition, he published nearly two hundred short stories in such family and women's magazines as *Home Circle, Yankee Blade, The Flag of Our Union,* and *Gleason's Literary Companion* during his career. Most of these pieces were also originally written prior to his success in the juvenile genre, however, and later reprinted in various publications. Finally, late in his life, after establishing his reputation as a writer of juvenile books, he composed three more adult novels, one of which remains unpublished and in manuscript.

This complete body of work, particularly the short apprenticeship pieces, still awaits a more thorough analysis than is possible here; however, a few representative adult works provide a context apart from the juvenile fiction for examining Alger's thought, clearly demonstrating that an important theme in his work has usually been overlooked because of the emphasis on the motif of success. Fortunately, Alger's thematic concerns in his adult fiction were so limited that it is not necessary to engage critically the entire corpus. The selections to be considered in this chapter, recurrently depicting the thematic contrast of Beauty and Money, clearly indicate that, instead of sanctioning the crass accumulation of wealth, Alger in all of his fiction consistently favored such prior claims as domestic harmony, the moral uses of money, and the selfless love of Art and Virtue.

I *Beauty versus Money*

In developing this crucial thematic contrast in his fiction, of course, Alger merely subscribed to the orthodoxy of the Harvard moral philosophers whose doctrines of Art and Beauty he had studied as a college student. According to the tradition of moral philosophy that Alger inherited, "moral beauty" was the most suitable subject of Art generally and didactic literature specifically. As Daniel W. Howe explains, antebellum Unitarian aesthetic theory "manifested the same preoccupation with preserving certainty and order that Unitarian ethical theory did," for the Harvard moralists endorsed "the Platonic doctrine that the perception of beauty is an intellectual recognition of harmonious interrelationships."[1] Indeed, in their view, aesthetics was a branch of ethics, and Andrews Norton, the so-called Unitarian pope, could declare *ex cathedra* that "there is nothing false in that splendid revelation of ancient philosophy that perfect goodness and perfect beauty are the same."[2] Aesthetic standards were considered analogous to moral principles. A writer in this tradition—as Alger was—accepted the important task of propagandizing for the Good—love of home, family, and country, charitable works such as helping the needy, rewarding the virtuous, attending the sick, and so forth—with the assurance that the product of his pen would be judged less on matters of style than on orthodoxy of content. Because the forms of moral beauty defied easy categorization, the Unitarian moralist wrote on the assumption that, as Alger suggested in his juvenile novel *Frank's Campaign* (1864), "the more we see of the beautiful, the better we are fitted to appreciate it in the wonderful variety of its numberless forms" (FC, 130–31).

An orthodox Unitarian, Alger would not have been pleased with fiction that only praised wealth-gathering, and he certainly would not have written such fiction himself. His crucial distinction between Beauty and Money, however, has usually been ignored. A persistent critical interpretation of the standard Alger story holds that the hero rises, if not from rags to riches, to at least a comfortable middle-class standard of living by exploiting every available opportunity to succeed financially. The hero's goal of wealth-in-abundance, according to this view, colors all of his thoughts and actions. Bruce E. Coad, for example, asserts that in his novels "Alger reflects an almost obsessive predilection for money-making."[3] Moses Ris-

chin in *The American Gospel of Success* similarly contends that
Alger's economic vision "followed logically from the Puritan ethic
which instructed man to lay up wealth for the greater glory of God."[4]
These critics suggest that Alger explicitly equated the pursuit of
happiness with the pursuit of wealth. They view the hero, in short,
as a mere fortune-hunter, his creator as a success ideologue, and
the novels as mere capitalist propaganda.

A dissenting interpretation of the standard Alger story, however,
holds that the hero is in fact a humanitarian rather than a ruthless
exploiter, and that he is rewarded in the denouement of each initiation novel for his acts of charity.[5] This interpretation, which suggests that the author was more concerned with morality and beauty
than with money, is supported by a reading of Alger's adult fiction.
To be sure, in the juveniles Alger did describe the increase of the
hero's bank account or detail the steps taken in the acquisition of
his birthright, but this moneymaking was symbolic of his initiation
into adulthood and was a badge of his innate moral goodness, con-
ferred by a benevolent patron who, like God, recognized his worth
and rewarded him. Because most of the virtuous characters in Alger's adult fiction already have been initiated, the importance of
money to them is drastically reduced, as might be expected on the
basis of this interpretation. Because Alger in his adult fiction labored
under no requirement to elevate his characters' stations as a sign
of their election, as was prescribed by the formula of his juveniles,
the wage-earning and monetary reward of the juvenile hero is re-
placed in the parallel structure of his adult fiction by courtship and
marriage among the mature characters. This correspondence between money in the juvenile fiction and marriage in the adult fiction
in turn suggests that Alger conceived of personal happiness as the
ultimate reward for moral behavior. The moral climate of Alger's
fictional world remains constant in both his adult and juvenile
works—a factor that enabled him to rewrite some of his adult works,
such as *Timothy Crump's Ward* and "Ralph Raymond's Heir," for
juvenile audiences. Indeed, the only apparent difference between
Alger's adult fiction and his juvenile fiction is the age of the characters he depicts, not the values these characters articulate and
embody. In other words, Alger's adult fiction, which develops the
theme of "Beauty versus Money," informs the myth he created in
his juvenile books by correcting the usual impression that he praised
wealth-gathering alone or considered it a sufficient end unto itself.

An adult story that Alger published in an 1859 issue of *Gleason's Weekly Line-of-Battle Ship* may be considered, in retrospect, a model for virtually all of his other adult fiction. Simply entitled "Beauty versus Money,"[6] the story describes the dilemma of genteel young Harry Mountford, whose father has arranged, without his knowledge or consent, for him to marry a rich heiress whom he has never seen. When the supposed heiress, Miss Graves, arrives at the Mountford estate in Scranton to visit her betrothed, Harry at once is attracted to her companion, a penniless seamstress named Miss Hamilton. Gradually, during the next several weeks, there dawns on Harry "a conviction that he was falling in love with Miss Hamilton. Certainly he had abundant reason. Not only was she far more attractive personally than the heiress, but she was also her superior in refinement and general culture." Although his father threatens to disown him, Harry proposes marriage to poor Miss Hamilton rather than to the well-heeled Miss Graves. Only after the wedding does the beautiful, cultured "seamstress" reveal that she had traded identities with the *real* seamstress "for the purpose of testing the disinterested love of Harry. This she had done with the happiest results." Forced to choose (or so he had believed) between Beauty and Money, Harry had opted for Beauty and incidentally obtained both. Employing the conventions of sentimental romance, the story culminates in a blissful marriage of deserving characters.

II *Early Adult Fiction*

This thematic contrast of Beauty and Money recurs in much of Alger's other adult fiction. In his first twelve adult novelle, written during a dozen years in the mid-nineteenth century, Alger clearly favored the claims of Beauty over those of Money.[7] Sentimental and melodramatic, these works describe a world in which the consequences of good and evil have been inexorably predetermined. The heroic characters strive not for fortune but for beatitudinal marital bliss. These works teach, as Alger concludes his early novel *Helen Ford*, that "Happiness must be earned; it can never be bought. To those who, like Helen, consecrate their lives to the noblest objects, and study to promote the happiness of all around them, the blessing comes unsought."[8] With no young heroes in transit struggling upward, the virtuous characters in these stories harbor few thoughts

of money, and on those rare occasions when virtuous characters do
think of money, they reveal their (and Alger's) low estimation of its
worth relative to the value of Beauty. In *Helen Ford*, for example,
a struggling artist complains to his friend and eventual lover Helen
that "it is money that rules the world. Before its sway we must all
bow, willing or unwilling. It is the want of money that drives me
to abandon that which is the chief joy of my life. . . . [Painting] will
gratify my aesthetic tastes; it will give me that which my soul craves;
it will open to me a world of beauty in which I can revel; but, alas!
it will not give me bread."[9] In contrast, evil characters in these
early stories covet filthy lucre and its perverse sexual correlate,
seduction.

In the tradition of melodrama, the virtuous characters in these
works inevitably are rewarded (by marriage, not necessarily by
wealth) and the evil characters inevitably punished. For example,
the hunchbacked, mercenary villain in Alger's early serial "Hugo,
the Deformed" commits suicide rather than suffer arrest for kidnapping the chaste heroine, while the romantic hero and his betrothed at length "attain that peaceful and tranquil happiness which
mutual love can alone bestow."[10] In his novella *Ralph Raymond's
Heir,* moreover, the two criminals who temporarily deprive an heir
of his modest birthright and who hope to appropriate it for themselves die in a grisly murder-suicide similar to the violent end of
"Hugo" (RRH, 211). The sordid quest for personal profit is righteously condemned by Alger in every instance. Without exception,
characters who are guilty of avarice are portrayed as miserable. For
example, at the end of "Manson the Miser" Alger depicts old Peter
Manson as he dies with "a few gold pieces firmly clutched in his
grasp. He had received a sudden summons" while engaged Scrooge-
like in counting his fortune.[11] Justice is meted out in this fictional
world not on a sliding scale of monetary gain or loss; rather, goodness
is rewarded with happiness and evil is punished with spiritual and/or
legal conviction or death. These works, in short, belie the interpretation of Algerism as unbridled capitalism, and suggests that
Unitarian minister Alger believed, as he wrote in the preface to his
juvenile novel *Sink or Swim* (1870), that "the consciousness of well-
doing . . . itself is a rich reward" (SorS, viii).

Also during these early years of his writing career Alger frequently
published short fiction for adults that, by contrasting Beauty and
Money, offered quaint moral lessons. A volume of his short tales,

entitled *Bertha's Christmas Vision: An Autumn Sheaf* (1856), was in fact Alger's first published book.[12] Most of his short pieces, however, appeared in magazines and were not collected. Of Alger's nearly two hundred adult stories, perhaps the best five appeared in four major magazines—*Putnam's, Graham's, Harper's Weekly,* and *Harper's Monthly*—and merit brief, individual attention.

Alger wrote one of his best early tales, "Love," for the original *Putnam's* magazine shortly before it suspended publication during the economic crisis of 1857.[13] This story sympathetically details the struggle of a young female protagonist who is robbed of her suitor by a mercenary "friend," yet who lives so selflessly that eventually she is rewarded providentially with a loving husband. Love Brainerd, a tenant in Achsah Root's house until she is asked to pay an exorbitant rent (love vs. the root of evil?), leaves her home in order to earn her living in a factory. Meanwhile, the unfeeling Achsah toys with the affections of Jim Whitman, who theretofore had courted only Love. Spurned by him, Love still remains faithful to those who have so ill treated her. When a blind singing master comes to her town, Love begins to "feel as if God had sent him to me, and spoken about it. . . . Nobody cares for him but me, and I should make him so happy. What am I good for but to spend and be spent for somebody? and who needs it more than he?" So "the Lord rewarded her in this world" with a happy marriage.

A second Alger adult tale, entitled "Five Hundred Dollars" (1858), essentially rebuts the allegation that the climate of Alger's world was always favorable to fortune-hunting, for in it the author acknowledges the moral snare always implicit in the urge to acquire wealth.[14] Gregory Flint, the narrator of this retrospective tale, explains to the reader that a few years earlier his late aunt had bequeathed to him five hundred dollars, and that immediately he had begun to search for an appropriate investment for his legacy. "There was something exhilarating in the idea of being a capitalist—with money to invest," he recalls. One morning Flint had met a "sleek personage, of very plausible address" whose name was Lynx. This mysterious stranger told Our Gullible Hero about an investment that he had recommended to a friend, with which, he explained, his friend had realized a fortune of twenty thousand dollars after only two years. Flint had calculated that "at that rate my five hundred dollars would have become fifty thousand." The mode of investment, Lynx explained, was quite simple: " 'I purchased for him a quarter section in a rising town in Minnesota.' " Supposedly, the purchased land had been acquired for building lots, so its value soared. Lynx also had assured him that such an opportunity was not unique, and that his advice would insure success. Flint remembers that "my imagination set fire at once. No more chance of my letting out my aunt's legacy at a paltry six per cent, when such golden harvests were to be had for the gathering." As a result, within the hour Flint had purchased from Lynx one hundred and sixty acres in Constantinople, Minnesota. The cost of the land, plus the commission that Flint paid the stranger, exhausted the five-hundred-dollar bequest. Flint had walked home "with the broad consciousness that I was a landed proprietor, and on the high road to fortune." Here, perhaps, the later Alger juvenile novel would end, for the benevolent patron who had "placed more than one young man with small means on the road to fortune" seemingly again had accomplished his self-appointed task. In two or three years, Flint had anticipated, he would be prosperous enough to offer a comfortable living to his intended wife, the lovely Julia Mackintosh.

Flint's vain aspirations are, of course, built on sand, for the mysterious stranger had deceived him. Two years later he had traveled to Minnesota to visit his claim, spending his nights in rude log huts, until finally he arrived at his village destination—"three miserable log-houses, in front of one of which a pig was rooting very composedly." Half of his quarter section, he then had learned, was swampland and the other half uncleared forest. In short, like later investors during the Florida land boom of the 1920s, he had lost his money. Flint returned from this journey "with all my daydreams effectually dispelled. I am quite as far from marrying Julia Mackintosh as ever. The revenues of my Western property will scarcely justify me in assuming so expensive a responsibility."

Although this apprenticeship piece introduces dramatic contrivances Alger would subsequently employ in his juvenile novels, the plot itself is an inversion of the success stories. On the one hand, there appear such devices as the confidence man who robs or bilks Our Hero, the pilgrimage to the West (a device used by Alger especially after his own first journey to California in 1877), and the hero's investment in land at the direction of a patron. No less than in his later juvenile fiction, Alger instructs his readers in a moral lesson—a modern, secular equivalent of the biblical parable of the Prodigal Son. On the other hand, the protagonist of this story is victimized by his passion for easy money and, unlike the heroes of the juvenile books, he sinks to destitution and bachelorhood instead of rising to respectability. In this way Alger expressly cautioned against money-hungering. The worldly invitation to rise to a higher economic station could be revoked, Alger averred, for the pristine innocence of people had been corrupted by the Original Sin of avarice.

In a third story, "Farmer Hayden's Thanksgiving-Day" (1863), Alger personified Beauty and Money as two suitors for the same woman and in this way contrasted their respective claims to her hand.[15] As the story opens, young Mary Hayden's father is threatened with foreclosure on his farm's mortgage by cruel Squire Hastings. But, if Mary will agree to marry him, he will allow her family to remain in their home. On her part, Mary is prepared to sacrifice herself to a fate worse than death: "If Mr. Hastings will not forego his cruel purpose on any other condition than that I become his wife, I am ready to consent." Her father, though tempted to accede, refuses to allow her self-sacrifice: "Better that we wander homeless but united in affection than give you as wife to that man. The thought that you had sacrificed yourself to him would embitter my existence. No, much as I value the old homestead, let it go, so that I keep my child." Fortunately, the night before the note falls due, an old admirer of Mary's, John Patten, returns to the village after several years at sea during which he has acquired modest wealth. Unrecognized by the farmer and his daughter, Patten offers to lend "the money to cancel the mortgage." Farmer Hayden accepts the offer only after he is certain that Patten expects nothing in return except an invitation to their Thanksgiving dinner and the satisfaction of thwarting Hastings' evil designs. After paying his debt and dismissing the squire from his home the next morning, Farmer Hayden "craved a blessing, and in the hearts of all there was a deep sense of gratitude to God, who had indeed made this a day worthy of thanksgiving." Two weeks later, John and Mary are married "in presence of the whole village, every man, woman, and child turning out to witness the ceremony." Happily, the squire's covetous motives have been frustrated by the disinterested love of John Patten, who is an instrument of divine intercession. The triumphant, virtuous characters obtain the bliss guaranteed in this fictional world by homestead and hearth.

Alger's fourth major story for adults, "Job Warner's Christmas"

(1863), was obviously inspired by, and nearly plagiarized from, Dickens's *A Christmas Carol*.[16] It describes the pathetic predicament of an assistant bookkeeper in the counting room of Bentley and Co. and his family as they prepare to celebrate the holiday on his modest salary. Although the Warners are poor, Alger explains, "there were few happier or more thankful hearts than those of the shabby book-keeper and his good wife." Still, economic hardship in the Warner home has been increased by Civil War-induced inflation. Necessities have become expensive and "made a rigid economy needful. Months ago the family had given up sugar, and butter was only used on Sunday." Rather than asking for a holiday from work as had Bob Cratchit, Job asks his employer for a small raise to compensate him partially for his lost purchasing power. Pennywise Mr. Bentley agrees only to consider the matter, and Job's wish to buy a few gifts for his family on this Christmas Eve seems doomed to frustration. Nevertheless, Job offers to help a street urchin who appeals to him for aid as he walks home. He exclaims, "I am poor, my child, but not so poor as you, thank God! I had intended to buy some little presents for my children, but they will be better pleased if I spend the money in making you comfortable." Employer Bentley overhears Job's offer, and he in turn resolves to become more charitable himself, to turn from Money to Beauty. He is, after all, "Not naturally a selfish man, only inconsiderate. Now that his benevolent impulses were excited, he would not rest till they were embodied in action." The upshot of this resolution is that Bentley swears off frugality. He increases Job's salary from seven hundred to a thousand dollars per year, and he grants Job and his wife an additional two hundred dollar annual allowance to care for the orphan found begging on the street. He accounts for his newfound benevolence by explaining to them that "prosperity had begun to harden my heart. At any rate it had made me thoughtless of the multitudes who are struggling with ills which my wealth can alleviate." The earlier, unredeemed Bentley is the prototype of the callous capitalist who stalks Alger's world in the juvenile books; the stock character's conversion in this tale, however, attests to Alger's abiding faith in the efficacy of good works and selflessness in a world sullied by war and privation. Predictably, Warner spends part of his new-won good fortune on gifts. With no Tiny Tim to squeak the final words, the story closes instead with a benediction from the gospel of Luke, read aloud by Warner to his family: "Glory to God in the highest, and on earth peace, good-will to men!" Without question, Alger's ministerial training shaped the moral caliber of his tales.

"Ralph Farnham's Romance" (1864), a fifth major adult story by Alger, concerns the hero's struggle to become a renowned author of beautiful, morally uplifting stories rather than a rich man.[17] Ralph journeys to the small town where the tale is set in order to write a romance. He hopes, as he writes to his sister, to earn enough by his pen only "to provide a home for you, however humble, so that we might be again united." If only that would happen, he "should feel happy." However, his interests are strictly literary, not commercial; he clearly favors the claims of Beauty over those of Money. Indeed, he comes to the village after rejecting an offer of a secure clerking position in the city, although he begins to doubt the wisdom of his decision. "Though it would bind me to a life I detest, it would have given me a secure income, while now I may only experience mortifying failure. . . . *I must succeed!*" Success is associated here not with income, but with artistic achievement. Significantly, Ralph has rejected exactly the type of position that constitutes the hero's reward in many of the juvenile novels. This adult story therefore may be considered as a subsequent chapter in the story of a hero who is offered a monetary reward for a kind deed but politely refuses it in order to stake his claim to the Good Life of Beauty.

Ralph, who boards near the mansion of Judge Henderson, the town magistrate, one day saves the life of the judge's daughter Ellen. As a reward for his rescue of the distressed heroine, he becomes a frequent guest in the judge's home. Through the intervention of the grateful Ellen, Ralph also becomes a weekly columnist for the local newspaper, which enables him to stave off starvation while he completes his romance. At length, Ralph and Ellen are betrothed, and their wedding date is set to coincide with the date that Ralph's manuscript is to be published. Ellen's father pronounces the benediction upon the happy couple—with whom Ralph's sister will come to live—when he tells Ralph, "You have talent, and Ellen has money. . . . It is a fair exchange." In other words, success in the story's terms is not prosperity, but the contentment assured by the happy coincidence of artistic achievement, marriage, and economic security.

Although each of these several adult stories speaks individually to the question of what Beauty and Money mean in the Alger canon, the author developed in them common themes that clarify his ap-

praisal of fortune-hunting. All of them promote the biblical virtues
of economy and charity, not entrepreneurship. For example, Gregory Flint is the man who squandered his legacy in foolish living,
in contrast to the wise economy of Ralph Farnham and Job Warner.
Economy is practiced by these characters not to raise investment
capital, but to satisfy the biblical injunction to be a faithful steward
of God's bounty and to alleviate suffering in the world. Moreover,
because the Warners are willing to share their livelihood, meager
as it may be, with the orphan, they become the exemplars of this
faith that converts thrifty Bentley into a fount of generosity. In this
world, especially in "Love," "Job Warner," and "Farmer Hayden,"
charity is practiced in order to reduce the suffering of the less
fortunate, to act upon Christ's command to "do unto others as you
would have them do unto you." Although it is not the social Dar-
winists' world of cutthroat competition, neither is it always a bright,
innocent world. On its fringes appear "street Arabs," orphaned and
hungry children in the supposed land of milk and honey, unfaithful
friends, and covetous squires. Finally, three stories in which the
protagonist plans to marry reveal Alger's deliberate use of irony.
Ralph Farnham, who seeks artistic success, is rewarded with it, a
bride, and financial security; Love Brainerd, who desires a happy
home, providentially is granted her wish. However, Gregory Flint
who, like Squire Hastings, seeks crass wealth and a bride, receives
neither. The difference between "Ralph Farnham" and "Love" on
one hand and "Five Hundred Dollars" on the other is that Ralph's
and Love's ambitions are honorable and their rewards deserved,
whereas Gregory Flint is motivated by greed and passion and exerts
no effort of his own by investing his inheritance in distant land on
a sham promise of wealth. All of them merit their fates. Like the
God of the Old Testament, Alger dispenses rewards and punish-
ments in absolute terms.

III   *Adult Fiction in Mid-Career*

After his initial success with *Ragged Dick* in 1868, Alger wrote
juvenile novels almost exclusively—often as many as four or five in
a single year—until his death in 1899. Upon three occasions, however, he returned to writing fiction for an adult audience. These
later works command particular attention, for they silhouette Alger's
mind long after the exigencies of his literary apprenticeship and

suggest that he continued to favor the claims of Beauty over those of Money throughout his writing career. In the first of these three novels written in the style of the newer genteel sentimentalism, *The New Schoolma'am; or, A Summer in North Sparta* (1877), Alger praised the life of self-sacrifice, of giving rather than receiving.[18] The heroine, wealthy debutante Mabel Frost Cunningham, scorns her class privilege in genteel New York society, assumes the name Mabel Frost, and comes with the airy grace of the ingénue to the village of North Sparta, New Hampshire, to teach in the middle school there. Alger explains her motives by insisting that sheer wealth is a curse, her bugbear: "Why had Mabel Frost given up a life of luxury to teach in a grammar school in an obscure country town? Young, beautiful, wealthy, but almost without family ties, she had wearied of the slavery of fashion. Young as she was, she had begun to know its hollowness. She sought an object and an interest in life. She felt that thus far she had lived only for herself. She formed the determination to live, in part at least, for others, and to take her share of the world's work" (16). Mabel performs her pedagogical tasks well and succeeds "in inspiring an interest in study such as had not been known before. She offered to teach a class in French and one in Latin, though it entailed extra labor" (47). Alger's choice of a teaching career for his heroine evinces his belief that a classical or humanistic education, "the birthright of every citizen" (33), would aid in the amelioration of social problems and was a prerequisite of personal advancement. As he wrote in his juvenile novel *Fame and Fortune* (1868), "You may depend upon it that a good education is the best preparation for an honorable and useful manhood" (Fa&F, 45). In this regard, Alger dissented from the opinions expressed by such entrepreneurs as Andrew Carnegie and John D. Rockefeller, who recommended that aspiring young men obtain technical or vocational training.

One other reference in this novel may serve to distinguish Alger's attitude about wealth and its prerogatives from the attitude expressed by the wealthy class and its religious apologists. The year of the novel's composition, 1877, was one of the most violent in the history of the labor movement in America. In fact, labor unions at this time were usually criticized by capitalists and religious leaders for allegedly interfering with the natural laws governing the marketplace. In an article for his own religious periodical, *Christian Union*, dated August 1, 1877, one of the most eminent ministers of the period, Henry Ward Beecher, invoked divine authority to decry the unchristian activities and expectations of the laboring class: "It is said that a dollar a day is not enough for a wife and five or six children. No, not if the man smokes or drinks beer. It is not enough if they are to live as he would be glad to have them live. It is not enough to enable them to live as perhaps they would have a right to live in prosperous times. But is not a dollar a day enough to buy bread with? Water costs nothing; and a man who cannot live on bread is not fit to live."[19] Alger was composing his novel at the same time that Beecher's celebrated comments were published. He may have read them (in 1870, at any rate, the *Christian Union* had published a review of Alger's *Ben the Luggage Boy*) or at least heard about them, for in his novel he has Mabel Frost Cunningham, who is to be paid at the rate of a dollar a day as a teacher, muse, "So I am to earn seven dollars a week . . .—I who never earned a dollar in my life; I am afraid I should not find it easy to restrict my expenses within that limit." Alger apparently shared the belief that a dollar per day was hardly sufficient to support a working class family, if strict economy would be necessary for a single young lady to maintain herself on that salary, and thus seemed to sympathize with the demands of labor.

Mabel eventually is repaid amply for her self-sacrifice, although not in dollars. She meets the mature version of Our Hero, artist Allan Thorpe, who recognizes her from a reception he had attended in New York several social seasons earlier, and she falls in love with him. On his part, Thorpe writes to a friend (Alger often employed even in his juvenile novels the epistolary technique for entering the mind of a character) that "between the struggling artist and the wealthy heiress there was a distance too great to be spanned even by love, but now that her estate is on a level with my own I need not hesitate. The same spirit that has enabled her to meet and conquer adversity will sustain her in the self denial and self sacrifice to which she may be called as the wife of a poor man. I have resolved to put my fortune to the test" (111). Social status is an artificial barrier among people, Alger implies, for the success of Thorpe's suit is not dependent upon Mabel's social station. Thorpe proposes marriage to the princess-in-disguise just before she reveals, much as had the seemingly poor seamstress "Miss Hamilton" in Alger's "Beauty versus Money," that they will not need to grovel for their livelihood. When Thorpe asks why, if still rich, she has become a schoolmarm, she replies, "Because I wished to be of some service to my kind; because I was tired of the hollow frivolity of the fashionable world. I don't regret my experiment. I never expected to be so richly rewarded" (138). A happy marriage is again the reward of the virtuous.

An unhappy union is the deserved punishment of two other characters in a subplot that ratifies Mabel's decision to flee the superficialities of fashionable society. After his own condescending proposal to the "poor" Mabel is refused, Randolph Chester, the middle-aged version of Alger's juvenile snob, marries a woman whom he ironically believes to be very rich, but who is "in truth, considerably straitened" (95). Marriage again is the vessel dispensing justice, for by their irrevocable unhappiness together Randolph and his wife are penalized for their snobbery and aristocratic pretensions.

The second of Alger's later three adult novels, entitled "Mabel Parker; or The Hidden Treasure. A Tale of the Frontier Settlements," was never published, and a manuscript copy of it has only recently come to light.[20] Transcribed in a copyist's hand with corrections by Alger himself, the manuscript was submitted to the publishing firm of Street and Smith in about 1878.[21] Its rejection by their editors may be explained by Alger's earlier unpopularity among adults (Street and Smith were publishers of the New York *Sun*, and would have been familiar with the situation); by their fear that, if successful, Alger would abandon the more lucrative juvenile market; or by the slow book trade of the late 1870s. These occasional forays into adult fiction, in any event, were not to be encouraged by his publishers.

The plot of "Mabel Parker" is hardly distinguishable from that of other sentimental romances of the period; its most salient feature is a thinly disguised similarity to James Fenimore Cooper's *The Pioneers*, which might have been yet another reason that Street and Smith declined to issue it.[22] Set in the lake region of central New York State around 1820, the story is basically another variation on the seduction theme then popular.[23] It does contain an Alger boy-hero, a swarthy lad named Zack, but in a subordinate role. The central conflict pits the villain, Dick Clarke, who attempts to extort from the widowed Squire Parker permission to wed his beautiful daughter Mabel, against the honorable, handsome, Harvard-educated Henry Davenport, Mabel's true love. "A selfish as well as a proud man,"[24] Parker is tempted to accede when he is promised the recovery of half of his inheritance, some fifty thousand dollars, by the perverse Clarke, who had discovered its location by accidentally finding a letter addressed to the squire from his father. The junior Parker had wasted the other half of his wealth in riotous living, although his daughter seems none the worse for it. The work also contains a subplot: in the Indian village near the settlement, another love triangle is resolved when Indian John, a malevolent, stereotypically drunken Indian who apparently is named after Indian John/Chingachgook of *The Pioneers*, is expelled from the tribe. As a result of the removal of his rival, the brave Okanoga wins the hand of beautiful squaw Waurega, daughter of the chief. The resolution of this subplot thus foreshadows the resolution of the main one. In an encounter of unworthy suitors in the forest, exiled Indian John steals Clarke's purse, which contains the intercepted letter. That letter is in turn found by young Zack and presented to the gallant Henry Davenport. The rightful heir thereby recovers his lost fortune without Clarke's help, and Mabel and Henry are wed with the squire's blessing.

Explicit in this novel is the admission that money is neither necessary nor sufficient for human well-being. The quest for fortune alone, Alger observes, is irrelevant to the larger questions of human happiness. Like a despicable snob from one of Alger's juvenile books grown to adulthood, Mabel's father receives his inheritance and lives a life of unmerited leisure. With neither guile nor rapacity, Mabel also becomes rich, deservedly so according to the determinism that steadfastly governs the lives of the virtuous in Alger's world, but she would willingly have spurned material wealth to insure happiness, and indeed she carefully distinguishes between the two states. As she tells her father, "I care not for money. To me it is of no value compared with the happiness which I shall enjoy as Henry's wife" (93). Even the villain Clarke has "the good taste to value youth and beauty above the mere dross of gold" (61); otherwise, he would have kept the missing treasure for himself.

Like the other sympathetic characters in Alger's adult fiction, those in this drama cherish not wealth but home and family. This novel is unique, however, for its increasingly complex economic and moral vision. Goodness and evil have become less distinct moral categories for Alger, and Clarke and Squire Parker inhabit that widening gray zone between virtue and depravity. The incongruity of Parker's undeserved wealth indicates, as Alger explicitly admitted in a juvenile novel written at about the same time, that "Plenty of mean men prosper" (BR, 154). In short, Alger was not an unequivocal proponent of business success. He found it necessary to qualify his earlier, reductive determinism that equated goodness with success and evil with failure in order to account for both the success of the undeserving and the poverty of the virtuous. Rebate scandals, investigations of trusts and monopolies, and exposés of child labor abuses convinced him that the phrase " 'business is business' " was "used to excuse all manner of vile acts" (AGP, 241). Morality, not money, remained his chief concern.

Alger's final adult work, *The Disagreeable Woman: A Social Mystery* (1895), the first new adult work by Alger to appear in nearly two decades, was published under the pseudonym Julian Starr, which may account in part for the little attention paid it. Only two known copies of the book survive.[25] Narrated from the point of view of a young physician, Dr. Fenwick, who has recently moved to New York from a small village in order to partake of the "wider opportunity" available to him in the city, the story involves a group of characters at his boarding house and is modeled closely after the Breakfast Table books of Oliver Wendell Holmes. Alger's last, unsuccessful attempt to broaden his audience, the novel thematically explores the sinister city and the irony of its purported "wider opportunity," especially during the economic depression that followed the Panic of 1893. One resident of the house, a young clerk at Macy's department store, for example, finally returns to her "country house and is now the wife of her rustic admirer." According to the narrator, whose insight anticipates that of Theodore Dreiser in *Sister Carrie*, she has chosen wisely, for "life in the great stores is a species of slavery, and she could save nothing from her salary" (26).

The doctor also ponders his own commitment to the city, as he recalls that "in the country village, where I knew everybody, I always looked forward to [Sunday] as the pleasantest day of the week. Here in the crowded city, I felt isolated from human sympathy" (17). The doctor often complains about his failure to become financially self-supporting in the city, and he particularly resents the selfish members of the upper class. "Rich men with large incomes keep [doctors] out of their pay for a long time," he observes (15). However, when one resident criticizes the doctor for wasting his time with charity cases, arguing that he "will never get rich in that way," Fenwick responds, "I do not expect to. I shall be satisfied if I can make a living" (20).

Clearly more interested in moral beauty than money and forever charitable, the doctor ministers to a distressed family whose poverty is enforced by the low wages offered by city employers. He prescribes rest and wholesome food, but is unable to give them any money because he has too little of his own, so on their account he appeals to another boarder in his house, the Disagreeable Woman. Although she is considered by the other residents to be a callous, indifferent woman, the doctor realizes that she merely scorns their frivolities; he knows that at heart she is a charitable, cultured woman to whom money is important only as a means to help others. "Under a brusque exterior she certainly possesses a kind heart, and consideration for others," the doctor says of her. "Upon everything in the shape of humbug or pretension she is severe, but she can appreciate worth and true nobility. In more than one instance I have applied to her in behalf of a poor patient, and never in vain" (26). Because she privately volunteers money to help the doctor's needy patients, because her charity is disinterested, she too is eventually rewarded. In the novel's final chapter, she learns from Fenwick of the illness of her long-lost fiancé, and Evangeline-like she attends his sickbed. When she finally is told that her patient will survive, "a look of grateful joy lighted up the face of the Disagreeable Woman" (28). The final Alger novel for adults ends, like most of its predecessors, with a long-deferred marriage on the verge of consummation.

This novel, like Alger's other adult works, supports the view that in Alger's fictional world happiness is earned by acts of charity and other forms of moral behavior, and that money is at best only an accessory of success. Moreover, the city as a setting is not depicted here as an Elysian Field of unlimited opportunity, but as a festering sore of social depravity, a stain on the social fabric. The same sense of the city often is conveyed in Alger's novels for juveniles. For example, in *Julius, or The Street Boy Out West* (1874), the hero must be transplanted from the city into the frontier before he can prosper. In *Joe's Luck* (1878), similarly, Alger admits that "a boy needs to be strong and self-reliant and willing to work if he comes [to the city] to compete for the prizes of life" (JL, 37). As in *Julius*, the hero of this novel abandons the brick and mortar mountains of the city for wider opportunities in the West.

This reading of Alger's adult fiction challenges the standard view of the world Alger created and the type of quest he described. The adult tales reveal by inference that Alger essentially wrote American morality fables, not business tracts or indiscreet celebrations of the American entrepreneur. The virtuous Alger protagonist invariably receives Good Fortune, but not necessarily wealth. His view thus must be contrasted with those of nineteenth-century clergymen who corrupted the traditional Protestant doctrine of the calling—which prescribed the stewardship duties of the man whom God had favored with worldly wealth—to sanctify mere wealth-getting and to justify the actions of the wealthy. Whereas the Right Reverend William Lawrence, Episcopal Bishop of Massachusetts and son of the successful industrialist Amos A. Lawrence, declared in 1901 that "Godliness is in league with riches,"[26] Alger dissented from this "theodicy of good fortune." "Sometimes the richest are the meanest," one of his juvenile heroes astutely observes (BR, 7). Never an apologist for the robber barons of the Gilded Age, Alger set his fiction in an earlier, seemingly simpler, pre-industrial era, and always was more concerned with the moral uses of money than with money itself. In the Alger canon, money may be a means to attain success, but it never constitutes success by itself. Rather, the hero earns success and happiness by his virtue, especially by his charity, and never by business acumen. A character who covets wealth or his neighbor's wife-to-be usually receives his just reward. Occasionally in his later novels, Alger described a world of more complex economic transactions in which the undeserving frustrate the Fates and gain wealth. "The wicked are sometimes prospered in this world," notes the wise guardian of one Alger boy hero. Still, as he continues, "This world is not all" (CC, 12). Nearing the end of his life, seasoned by his knowledge that unethical business practices in a foreboding real world often reward the culprits, Alger appealed for an eschatological vindication of the moral principles that animate his fictional world.

CHAPTER 4

The Moral Foundation of the Juvenile Fiction

I Alger's Theory of Juvenile Fiction

DURING his career Alger routinely wrote thousands of words in a single day, and once composed an entire juvenile book in only two weeks.[1] Although he often claimed that his inspiration came from real boys "in order that my characters might seem to be drawn from life,"[2] on other occasions he admitted that "I never fully understand a character, to begin with, but gradually become acquainted with it as I go on. The characters, once introduced, gradually develop and in turn shape the story."[3] Despite his rapid composition and seemingly slipshod technique, however, Alger was more than a mere hack writer of potboilers. Indeed, he consciously embraced a definable theory of juvenile fiction which, while not new, sheds light on his purpose in writing and on his own understanding of the influence of his books.

In a late essay, one of the last pieces he prepared for publication before his retirement in 1896, Alger discussed the potential influence—for good *or* ill—that a writer for boys may exert upon his impressionable readers, and claimed that "the influence of no writer for adults can compare with his." Because Alger, like other Harvard Unitarians, accepted the traditional view of the artist as a moral and religious teacher, he argued that especially a writer for boys "should remember his responsibility and exert a wholesome influence on his young readers. Honesty, industry, frugality, and a worthy ambition he can preach through the medium of a story much more effectively than a lecturer or a preacher." Carefully separating his characters into sheep and goats, Alger clearly expressed his own opinions through the coloring he gave their speeches. Unlike rounded characters in more realistic fiction, the virtuous hero and his allies in these books often speak for the author in defense of the

Good, and the villains arrayed against them offer intentionally sophistic justifications for Evil. Like other moralists who worried about the corrupting influence of popular novels, Alger cautioned against the insidious influence of cheap juvenile fiction. "Sensational stories, such as are found in the dime and half-dime libraries, do much harm, and are very objectionable. Many a boy has been tempted to crime by them. Such stories as 'The Boy Highwayman,' 'The Boy Pirate,' and books of that class, do incalculable mischief."[4]

Not surprisingly, Alger expressed similar views in his novels—which, ironically, often were denounced during his life as too sensational. His virtuous heroes self-righteously deny ever reading dime novels, and when he had a boy admit to indulging in "some nice dime novel like 'The Demon of the Danube' " (YO, 54), he was merely indicating how far that particular character has to climb to reach respectability. Like one of his patrons who "belonged to the old school of moralists and looked with suspicion upon all works of fiction, with a very few exceptions" (YO, 54), Alger recommended that his readers read only instructive books in their leisure hours. The libraries of his heroes contain such works of fiction as *Pilgrim's Progress*, *Robinson Crusoe*, the novels of Scott and Dickens, and the juvenile works of Oliver Optic and Horatio Alger, Jr. In short, Alger offered his readers such heroes as Ragged Dick, who "would not steal, or cheat, or impose upon younger boys, but was frank and straight-forward, manly and self-reliant," because he hoped "they may find something in him to imitate" (RD, 43-44). He sought to "exert a salutary influence" upon his readers "by setting before them inspiring examples of what energy, ambition, and an honest purpose may achieve."[5]

II *Sources and Literary Models*

During the thirty-five years he wrote for boys, Alger rarely varied the formulaic plot and stock characterizations with which he filled his hundred and three juvenile books. Whether he was composing a boys' biography of Abraham Lincoln or another thin serial for *The Argosy*, Alger wrote according to the following general outline: A teen-aged boy whose experience of the sinister adult world is slight, yet whose virtue entitles him to the reader's respect, is cast unexpectedly into that sinister world and forced to struggle for a livelihood. At some point in this picaresque novel, the hero enters the

City, both a fabled land of opportunity and a potentially corrupting environment, where he meets an array of allies and confidence men. His exemplary struggle to maintain his social respectability, to clear his or another's name of false accusations, to gain a measure of economic independence from those stepmothers or squires who wish to oppress him—this is the substance of the standard Alger plot. Alger always offered a foil to his virtuous hero, usually a parochial snob who neither travels nor struggles, whose behavior is supremely selfish, who aspires to wealth, and who invariably ends the novel clinging to a rung lower on the social ladder than the one attained by the hero. At length, the hero earns the admiration of an adult patron who rewards him with elevated social station, usually a job or reunion with his patrician family, and the trappings of respectability, a watch and a new suit, which he flaunts before the deflated snob.

Although this outline served him for thirty-five years, it was itself an assimilation of two earlier literary models, and one to which Alger could adapt other models as well. His two most important formal models were Franklin's *Autobiography*, and the social novels of Dickens. Alger borrowed both his basic plot and symbols from the early pages of the *Autobiography*, to the point when young Ben returns to Boston from Philadelphia wearing a new suit and sporting a watch. Cleverly parodying the parable of the Prodigal Son, Franklin wrote that

My unexpected appearance surprised the family; all were, however, very glad to see me and made me welcome, except my brother. I went to see him at his printing house. I was better dressed than ever while in his service, having a genteel new suit from head to foot, a watch, and my pockets lined with near five pounds sterling in silver. He received me not very frankly, looked me all over, and turned to his work again.[6]

Just as Franklin described his apprenticeship in Philadelphia and triumphal return to Boston in the *Autobiography*, so did Alger typically allow his returned hero to deflate snobbish pretensions by walking the streets of his hometown wearing a new suit and displaying a watch. In *Struggling Upward* (1886), for example, the hero discomfits the snob in a scene reminiscent of Franklin's homecoming which, with only minor variations, recurs throughout Alger's juveniles:

On his way home from school Randolph was destined to be surprised. Not far from his own house he met Luke, arrayed in his new suit, with a chain that looked like gold crossing his waistcoat. Instead of looking confused and ashamed, Luke looked uncommonly bright and cheerful. Randolph was amazed. What could it all mean? He had intended not to notice Luke, but to pass him with a scornful smile, but his curiosity got the better of him. . . .

"Humph! You seem to have invested in a new suit."

"Yes; my old suit was getting decidedly shabby, as you kindly remarked." . . .

"I see you have a new watch-chain, too." . . .

"Yes; you may like to see my new watch." And Luke, with pardonable triumph, produced his new watch, which was a stem-winder, whereas Randolph's was only a key-winder. . . .

"You seem to have plenty of money," he said. (SU, 63,64)

As John Cawelti suggests, the hero's new suit "marks the initial step in his advancement, his escape from the dirty and ragged classes and his entry upon respectability," and his watch marks his "attainment of a more elevated position, and is a symbol of punctuality and his respect for time as well as a sign of the attainment of young manhood."[7]

Alger did not exhaust his interest in Franklin by recurrently depicting scenes from the *Autobiography* or employing a pair of symbols, however. Franklin's appeal during the Gilded Age was pervasive, as Louis B. Wright has explained, because "by a credible though partial perception" of Franklin's philosophy he became the "high priest of the religion of commercial success."[8] By offering Franklin as a model worthy of emulation, Alger paradoxically served his eighteenth-century didactic purpose and remained topical in the late nineteenth century. It is not surprising, then, that five of his heroes and two of his patrons are named Ben, one patron claims to be descended from Franklin, and even the name "Ragged Dick" seems less Alger's invention than a rephrasing of "Poor Richard." Three of Alger's heroes deliberately model their lives after Franklin, and three others directly quote his adages.

The importance of the Franklin model is most apparent in two volumes which Alger wrote in 1873–74—*Bound to Rise* and its sequel, *Risen from the Ranks*. These novels trace the rise of the hero, Harry Walton—who specifically patterns himself after the Franklin of the *Autobiography*—from poor New England farm boy

to newspaper editor and popular Congressman. As a prize for de-
claiming Daniel Webster's famous reply to Robert Y. Hayne, Harry
is awarded a copy of "the life of the great American philosopher and
statesman, Benjamin Franklin." His teacher tells him, "I hope you
will read and profit by it, and try like him to make your life a credit
to yourself and a blessing to mankind" (BR, 26). So Harry

began the story. . . . He was surprised to find that Franklin was a poor
boy, and had to work for a living. He started out in life on his own account,
and through industry, frugality, perserverance, and a fixed determination
to rise in life, he became a distinguished man in the end, and a wise man
also, though his early opportunities were very limited. It seemed to Harry
that there was a great similarity between his own circumstances and position
in life and those of the great man about whom he was reading, and this
made the biography the more fascinating. The hope came to him that, by
following Franklin's example, he, too, might become a successful man.
(BR, 27–28)

Inspired by Franklin, Harry convinces his parents that he too should
enter the adult world in quest of a niche, with such arguments as
"I don't believe Franklin was much older than I, and he got along"
(BR, 31). In all respects Harry models himself after the Franklin
about whom he reads: "It was the chart by which he meant to steer
in the unknown career which stretched before him. He knew so
little of the world that he trusted implicitly to that as a guide, and
he silently stored away the wise precepts in conformity with which
the great practical philosopher had shaped and molded his life" (BR,
35).

After meeting a deranged hermit who thinks that he is Andrew
Jackson (and who offers him Franklin's old post as Minister to
France), Harry enters a small town "with a roll in his hand, eating
an apple," much as Franklin entered Philadelphia for the first time
(BR, 55). Immediately he applies to the postmaster—a Franklin
figure—for information about work in the town. He enters the employ of a shoe manufacturer, and spends his evenings studying at
the public library—yet another Franklinesque trait—because he
"was growing ambitious. . . . Franklin, whom he had taken as his
great exemplar, didn't go to college; yet he made himself one of
the foremost scientific men of the age and acquired enduring reputation, not only as a statesman and a patriot, but chiefly as a
philosopher" (BR, 82–83). Harry envies Franklin's reputation as a
public servant, not his wealth, and he hopes eventually to become

an editor, so he applies for work at a printing shop. "I shouldn't expect to turn out a Franklin," he tells the shopowner, "but I think one couldn't help being improved by the business" (BR, 128). He is hired and earns enough to settle his father's debt with a squire who had threatened foreclosure. At this point, with Harry "still at the bottom of the ladder" (BR, 162), Alger closes the first of the two volumes.

The sequel opens with Harry entering the office of the *Centreville Gazette* as an apprentice printer, still harboring his ambition to become an editor. His employer introduces him as the "second Benjamin Franklin" (RfR, 6), a phrase Harry's envious co-workers soon adopt as an approbation. Resolving "to get some books and study a little every day . . . the way Franklin did" (RfR, 13), Harry meets a wealthy Boston patrician, a student at a local academy, who agrees to tutor him in French. Through his offices, Harry is elected to membership in and eventually to the presidency of the Clionian Society, an association of young intellectuals like Franklin's Junto. Encouraged in this forum to publish his ideas, Harry composes an essay, entitled "Ambition," which he signs with the *nom de plume* "Franklin" and submits to a Boston newspaper. Alger noted that even in this endeavor Harry "was influenced by the example of Franklin, who, while yet a boy in his teens, contributed articles to his brother's paper, though at the time the authorship was not suspected" (RfR, 66).

Under the pseudonym Frank Lynn, Harry soon acquires a considerable literary reputation, much as did Franklin in the "Silence Dogood" papers. Eventually, he succeeds the editor of the *Gazette*, is elected to the New Hampshire legislature a few months after obtaining his majority and to the U. S. Congress at the age of twenty-eight. A common Alger hero insofar as he "had never sought wealth," he is "content with a comfortable support and a competence." To be sure, "he was ambitious, but it was a creditable and honorable ambition. He sought to promote the public welfare and advance the public interests, both as a speaker and as a writer; and though sometimes misrepresented, the people, on the whole, did him justice" (RfR, 162–63). Presumably, like the first Franklin, he will grow old and honored among his countrymen.

Besides drawing on Franklin, Alger borrowed incidents, characters, and an authorial tone from Dickens. He ladled facts about the condition of the poor into his fiction because, as he observed, it is difficult to sympathize with the social outcasts without a "knowledge of how the poorest classes lived" (TT, 106). As a result, one critic suggests that his juvenile novels "comprise a valuable social documentation that is often reminiscent of Dickens."⁹ Certainly Alger planned his fiction to be partly incisive social commentary. The following passage, for example, owes its tone to Dickens and its content to a more obvious factual source, Dorothea Dix, who at mid-century had pioneered the investigation of conditions in Massachusetts asylums: "Mrs. Fogson led the way into a large room where sat the paupers, a forlorn, unhappy-looking company. Two of the ladies were knitting; one young woman, who had lost her child, and with it her mind, was fondling a rag baby; two were braiding a rag carpet, and others were sitting with vacant faces, looking as if life had no attraction for them" (JPB, 408). Alger apparently hoped to imitate Dickens's success in writing popular novels with a social purpose, though on the juvenile level. He often copied incidents and characters into his own fiction from four Dickens novels which feature a juvenile hero—*Great Expectations, David Copperfield, Nicholas Nickleby,* and *Oliver Twist.* For example, he introduced characters modeled after such Dickens characters as Wilkins Micawber in *The Young Outlaw* (1875). Sally Brass in *Hector's Inheritance* (1883), and Smike in *Grit* (1884). The Dickens work most often imitated by Alger, however, was *Oliver Twist,* which he once described as "Dickens's immortal story" (MMV, 236). No fewer than fourteen Alger juveniles employ *Oliver* twists in the plot, usually the discovery of a locket containing pictures used to identify the hero, who had been kidnapped as a baby, and to reunite him with his prosperous family. Alger also modeled other incidents in his juvenile fiction after other parts of the novel, as in *Paul Prescott's Charge* (1865), in which his hungry hero asks the stern mistress of a boarding school "for more":

"Please, ma'am," said he to Mrs. Mudge, "I should like some butter."

Paul's companions dropped their spoons in astonishment at his daring, and Mrs. Mudge let fall a kettle she was removing from the fire in sheer amazement.

"What did you ask for?" she inquired, as if to make sure that her ears did not deceive her.

"A little butter," repeated Paul, unconscious of the great presumption of which he had been guilty.

"You want butter, do you?" repeated Mrs. Mudge. "Perhaps you'd like a slice of beef-steak and a piece of plum-pudding, too, wouldn't you?" (PPC, 33-34)

Similarly, in *Adrift in New York* (1889) Alger transplanted the seedy Artful Dodger from the London slums to the New York slums, renamed him Tom Dodger, and converted him in the course of the novel from thief to respectable hero. And *The Young Explorer* (1880) contains a "brutal villain" whom other characters compare with Bill Sykes (YEx, 131). In short, Dickens's works, especially *Oliver Twist*, provided a rich source of incidents and characters for Alger's juvenile fiction, and in addition offered a model authorial tone toward these materials which Alger sought to imitate.

Alger also derived incidents and characters from many other sources, and it is clear that he carefully selected his models in order both to reduce sensationalism and to inspire an interest in respectable literature among his readers. The plots of *Brave and Bold* (1872) and *The Tin Box* (1882), for example, seem to be modernized versions of *The Odyssey* told from the point of view of Telemachus. Several Alger juveniles set at sea, among them *Facing the World* (1885) and *In Search of Treasure* (1894), borrow incidents from *Robinson Crusoe* and the sea tales of Richard Henry Dana and Herman Melville.[10] Especially in his "Pacific series" of juvenile novels set in the Old West (1878–82) and occasionally in other novels, Alger borrowed character and incident from James Fenimore Cooper's Leatherstocking tales, which he had read as a teenager. He also recast several of Mark Twain's novels for his juvenile audience, including *The Prince and the Pauper* in chapter XXVII of *Tom Brace* (1889) and *Huck Finn* in *Bob Burton* (1886–87). Predictably, Unitarian minister Alger often used the parables of Jesus as literary models for incidents in his didactic fiction, especially those of the Good Samaritan, the Prodigal Son, and the Ten Talents. And he borrowed incidents for his fiction from his reading in the *Atlantic Monthly*. Imitating Bret Harte in "The Poet of Sierra Flat" (*Atlantic*, July 1871), about a Western writer of doggerel verse, for example, Alger introduced in *Strive and Succeed* (1872) a comic Western poetess who complains about the discriminatory editorial policies of leading Eastern periodicals. In short, Alger was not only a formulaic writer, but an unoriginal one.

III *Literary Style and Themes*

Alger's books are usually considered literary museum pieces at least partly because of his anachronistic style. To be blunt, Alger's prose is often laughable. Although he was not a craftsman, he did put flesh on the bones of his literary theory with a style that was distinctive. In addition to his basic symbols of new clothes and a watch, Alger used houses as status symbols and even gave an occasional villain yellow tusks as symbols of his venality. He effectively foreshadowed plot action by using devices such as fortune-tellers and playscripts. Still, his style may be best distinguished from the style of pulp juveniles written in "fiction factories" by the quality of his literary allusions.

A didactic writer in two senses—as a moralist and as an educator— Alger drew from a greater variety of literary sources than any other writer for boys. Many of his sources are predictable. He alluded to the Bible, for example, in about half of his novels, and he quoted or mentioned each of the Fireside poets at least twice, his Harvard teacher Longfellow most often. Surprisingly, perhaps, he alluded to Shakespeare in nearly half of his juvenile books, and quoted Milton in *Phil the Fiddler* (1872). A defender of classical learning, Alger quoted from Cicero in *Bernard Brooks' Adventures* (1893) and Horace in *Walter Sherwood's Probation* (1890), and from several English neoclassical writers, including Joseph Addison in *Five Hundred Dollars* (1889-90), Oliver Goldsmith in *Dean Dunham* (1888), Thomas Gray in *Ralph Raymond's Heir* (1869), William Cowper in *The Young Musician* (1881), and Alexander Pope in *Andy Gordon* (1881). He even once referred to Pope's "Essay on Man" as "a poem which I fear is going out of fashion, which is certainly a pity, for apart from its literary merits it contains a great deal of sensible advice as to the conduct of life" (Farm, 34). Alger also quoted from such diverse sources as Robert Burns in *Adventures of a Telegraph Boy* (1886) and *Driven from Home* (1889), Thomas Paine in *Julius* (1874), and Tennyson in *Jack's Ward* (1875), and at various times alluded to Dante, Chaucer, Spenser, Dryden, Johnson, Watts, Wordsworth, Coleridge, Byron, Mill, Hugo, Voltaire, Goethe, and Schiller. Among his contemporaries he quoted Thomas Hood, Thomas Campbell, and the elder Henry James, and he referred to Carlyle, Emerson, Stowe, Howells, Stevenson, Edward Everett Hale, and Bayard Taylor. In *The Erie Train Boy* (1890) Alger even named a character Isabel Archer after the heroine of the junior Henry James's *The Portrait of a Lady*. By the diversity of his allusions, Alger, no mere hack writer, both revealed his erudition and enhanced the literary quality of his work.

Alger also treated a diversity of themes in his juvenile books,

unlike his singular concern with "Beauty vs. Money" in his adult
fiction. He developed six major themes in his juveniles, belying the
critical commonplace that all of his books were alike. The first
theme, the Rise to Respectability, was Alger's most important occasionally asserted even in his late books. As John Cawelti has
observed, "It is unfair to call [Alger] an uninhibited adulator of
wealth who equated spiritual grace with business success. The true
aim of the Alger hero is respectability, a happy state only partially
defined by economic repute."[11] In his preface to *Slow and Sure*
(1872) he mentioned explicitly the "rise to respectability" enjoyed
by his young heroes (Sl&S, 5), and as late as 1889, in both *A Boy's
Fortune* and *Adrift in New York*, he had his heroes articulate their
ambition to rise to a position of respect, not necessarily wealth. But
the best illustration of the Rise to Respectability in Alger appears
in his first and most popular success novel, *Ragged Dick, or Street
Life in New York* (1867). "I mean to turn over a new leaf, and try
to grow up 'spectable," the protagonist declares early in the book
(RD, 88). Even in his lowly position, Dick seems destined to rise.
Though poor, he is energetic and alert for business, and, Alger
noted, in the bootblacking trade as in "higher avocations, the same
rule prevails, that energy and industry are rewarded, and indolence
suffers" (RD, 46). After frustrating a dishonest clerk's attempt to
retain a gentleman's money in change, Dick is rewarded with the
task of guiding the man's nephew around the city. Before the tour,
his patron replaces Dick's ragged suit with a neat one, signaling the
beginning of his transformation from Ragged Dick into the respectable Richard Hunter, Esq. During his Baedeker-like tour of the
city, Dick thwarts a confidence game, exposes the tricks of a dishonest clothier, and is falsely accused of purse-snatching. Meanwhile, he has confessed to the nephew his ambition to become an
office boy and "learn business, and grow up 'spectable" (RD, 73).
Intuitively adult, the nephew responds, "If you'll try to be somebody, and grow up into a respectable member of society, you will.
You may not become rich,—it isn't everybody that becomes rich,
you know,—but you can obtain a good position, and be respected"
(RD, 75). His advice is echoed later by his uncle: "I hope, my lad,
you will prosper and rise in the world. You know in this free country
poverty in early life is no bar to a man's advancement. . . . Save
your money, my lad, buy books, and determine to be somebody,
and you may yet fill an honorable position" (RD, 108–09).

With the five dollars earned as a guide, Dick abandons his alley-way tenancy, hires a room, and charitably invites Henry Fosdick, a younger and weaker bootblack, to live with him. In exchange for Fosdick's tutelage in grammar and geography, Dick pays their entire rent. After acquiring a permanent residence, he next opens a savings account and begins to attend church, while Fosdick secures a clerking position. After a nine-month gestation, during which Dick and Fosdick have faithfully saved money, a fellow boarder and intemperate bartender steals Dick's bankbook. Dick traps the crook as he attempts an illegal withdrawal, and he is arrested. While at the bank, Dick withdraws enough money to save a friend's mother from eviction. By this time he has learned to read and write, and he seeks to leave bootblacking for a more respectable position in a counting house. One day, by chance, he rescues a child who had fallen overboard from a ferry. The grateful father offers Dick a position as clerk in his counting house at the munificent salary of ten dollars a week. Significantly, Dick admits that he would have worked for less than he had earned blacking boots. The status of respectability, not a high salary, completes his transition from Ragged Dick to Richard Hunter.

The recurrence in Alger's fiction of the theme of the Rise to Respectability underscores the inaccuracy of the widespread opinion that his heroes rise from rags to riches. Indeed, insofar as Alger's heroes prosper at all, they do so because they *deserve* prosperity, because they happily *earn* it with their virtue, however contrived the mechanism through which they obtain it. Daniel W. Howe explains that the Harvard moralists believed "God had provided for the recompense of virtue; the righteous would prosper here on earth and receive a heavenly reward as well."[12] As Alger restated the notion, "The best way to strive for success is to deserve it" (SorS, vii). Alger's heroes always merit their good fortune—an idea which, like respectability, is associated only tangentially to wealth.

A second major theme in Alger's juveniles is that characters can be Strengthened by Adversity. As Howe observes, the Unitarian theodicy taught "that suffering could be a useful device for character development. In consequence, there is a subordinate theme in praise of suffering which runs underneath the Unitarian chorus of joyful aspiration."[13] Alger echoed this theme in many of his novels, especially those like *Strong and Steady* (1871) and *Shifting for Himself* (1876) in which a hero born to wealth is "unexpectedly reduced from affluence to poverty, and compelled to fight his own way in life" (St&St, vii). Each of the eight volumes of the "Luck and Pluck series" (1869–75), thematically devoted "to the truth that a manly spirit is better than the gifts of fortune" (L&P, v), depicts a hero who is strengthened by adversity much as Alger hoped his readers would be. In 1876, with the national economy in the throes of a deep depression, Alger sought to comfort those readers who were suffering: "In the last three years many thousand American boys have been compelled . . . to give up their cherished hopes, and exchange school-life for narrow means and hard work. . . . I shall be glad if the story of Gilbert Greyson and his fortunes gives heart or hope to any of my young readers who are similarly placed. The loss of wealth often develops a manly self-reliance, and in such cases it may prove a blessing in disguise" (SH, vi). Alger feigned no pity for those born into the working class, for with his faith in upward mobility he believed that early hardship would promote their eventual success, not impede it: "Early trial and struggle, as the history of the majority of our successful men abundantly attests, tend to strengthen and invigorate the character" (L&P, v). The young Lincoln, for example, seemed to benefit from the "hardships of his lot. That is the way strong men are made" (BacB, 33). A poor boy should even consider his privation a blessing, Alger averred, for it may "give him that self-reliance of which the sons of rich men so often stand in need. . . . Let those boys who are now passing through the discipline of poverty and privation, take courage" (DN, 296).

Alger also adapted the theme of Beauty versus Money, which had been central to his adult fiction, to his juvenile novels. Generally, he developed the theme as he had in that apprenticeship work. Occasionally he affirmed the beauty of life over money, as in *Ralph Raymond's Heir* (1869): "Every day life is bartered for [money]; not always criminally, but sacrificed by overwork or undue risk, so insatiable is the hunger for gold, and so desperate are the efforts by which men seek to obtain it" (RRH, 101). Usually, however, he used pairs of characters broadly representative of the ideas of beauty and money in order to contrast them. In *The Train Boy* (1883) he reused the basic plot of *The New Schoolma'm*: the struggling artist, now named Frederic Vernon, meets the pretty ingenue, now Grace Dearborn (!). Providentially, "each discovered that the other had a mind rarely cultivated," and they fall in love. Eventually the "wealthy heiress" who "moves in the most exclusive society" marries Vernon, "an artist, a gentleman, and a man of talent" (TrB, 72, 114). In *The Erie Train Boy* (1890) Alger reused the formula of his adult story "Love," which prescribed that a poor-but-beautiful woman be wooed and won despite the wiles practiced on her suitor by a rich-but-depraved woman. And in *Ben's Nugget* (1882) he reused the basic plot of "Farmer Hayden's Thanksgiving-Day," in which a young woman resists the designs of a mercenary in order to marry her true love.

Alger also contrasted rural virtue and urban vice in his juvenile fiction. With this fourth theme, the Country versus the City, Alger adapted the nostalgic myth of the country boy as a moral exemplar to the modern notion of the city as sphere of economic opportunity. In his novel *Wait and Hope* (1877) Alger offered a succinct summary of his standard contrast of country and city: "While a large city has more temptations than a small town, it also has more opportunities for improvement" (W&H, 117–18). Though he modified the design of his stock hero as he groped for his métier, Alger retained this fundamental distinction, which was rooted in agrarian idealism, throughout his juvenile fiction. When the validity of the distinction was questioned in the 1920s by such figures as Sinclair Lewis and H. L. Mencken who announced an "escape from the village," the reputation of Alger and other celebrants of the country boy myth suffered accordingly.

For some of his earliest juvenile writing, as in *Paul Prescott's Charge* (1865), Alger invented heroes who are naive country bumpkins ill-equipped to swim in the tempestuous sea of the city. The sinful Babel simply overwhelms the innocent hero, who flees its temptations. For his most popular fiction, written in the late 1860s, Alger invented heroes who are street-wise urchins incongruously virtuous. Not even the small-town intimacy of the Newsboys' Lodging House can account fully for their village virtues. Finally, Alger invented mobile heroes who could both rise socially and traverse the gulf separating the disparate worlds of country and city. The hero of *Ben the Luggage Boy* (1870), for example, comes to New York from an outlying village only to sense an awful loneliness: "He felt that among the crowd of persons that jostled him as he stood at the corner, there was not one who felt an interest in him, or even knew his name. It was very different in his native village, where he knew everybody, and everybody had a friendly word for him. . . . The city had not proved the paradise he had expected

(BLB, 35, 73). Still, he eventually does prosper in his new surroundings. In this later fiction country boys suffer an interminable
period of adjustment to city ways, but eventually they do adjust.

True to the traditional country boy mythology, Alger believed,
as he wrote in *Chester Rand* (1892), that "it is country boys that
make the most successful men" (CR, 8). Nevertheless, he discouraged the rural poor from migrating to the city. Ignorant of the social
forces that herded the lower class from the country into cheap
tenement districts, Alger seemed only to realize that the plight of
these "cliff-dwellers" was complicated by their residence in the city:
"A stone's throw from Centre Street stands a tall tenement-house,
sheltering anywhere from forty to fifty families in squalid wretched-
ness. The rent which each family pays would procure a neat house
in a country town, with perhaps a little land beside; but the city
has a mysterious fascination for the poorer classes, and year after
year many who might make the change herd together in contracted
and noisome quarters, when they might have their share of light
and space in country neighborhoods" (TelB, 22). Alger strongly
discouraged his impressionable young readers, perhaps enticed by
the modest success enjoyed by the heroes of his urban novels, from
leaving their comfortable country homes for uncertain futures in
the city. "There is many a hard-working clerk of middle age, living
poorly, and with nothing laid by, in the city, who, had he remained
in his native village, might have reached a modest independence,"
he once observed (D&D, 72). He thus inferred that it is better to
earn a modest competency in a village than risk a livelihood in the
city—a conclusion that seriously undermines his reputation as an
ideologue of success. Indeed, in some of his later novels about a
socially and geographically mobile hero Alger even reversed the
expected journey of the hero from country to city, instead trans-
planting a stunted street Arab into more fertile country soil.

The best example of this plot-type appears in *Julius, or The Street
Boy Out West* (1874). On its first page, the orphan Julius tells
another street urchin about his plans to go West under the auspices
of the Children's Aid Society: "I'm goin' on to a farm, or into a
store, and grow up respectable" (Jul, 1). Julius's escape from these
vile surroundings to a foster home in the country, in Alger's view,
ought to be beneficial, for "the great city had been a harsh stepmother to him. He had suffered often from cold and hunger, during
the years that he had been drifting about her streets, an unconsid-

ered waif in the great sea of life. He had received kindness from few, harshness from many. From the age of five he had been forced to earn his own living" (Jul, 13). Although the program of orphan resettlement administered by the Society had been criticized for matching cruel foster parents with incorrigible boys who merely ran back to the city, Alger contended that the boys "are treated kindly almost without exception" (Jul, 28) and that "removed from the temptations and privations of the city, their better natures assert themselves, and they behave as well as ordinary children" (Jul, 29). Julius is also strengthened physically by his move to the country:

"When we first made acquaintance with Julius, in the streets of New York, he was meagre and rather undersized. Want and privation had checked his growth, as was natural. But since he had found a home in the West, he had lived generously, enjoyed pure air, and a sufficiency of out-of-door exercise, and . . . had grown three inches in height; his form had expanded; the pale, unhealthy hue of his cheek had given place to a healthy bloom, and his strength had considerably increased." (Jul, 78)

At novel's end, the adult Julius, now prosperous and engaged to be married, visits New York and exhorts the residents of the Lodging House "to leave the city streets, and go out West. . . . If you want to prosper, and grow up respectable, I advise you to come out as soon as you get the chance" (Jul, 146). Confident that only exceptional boys could struggle upward in the city in the manner of Ragged Dick, Alger urged his readers to rise to respectability in the country, and warned them that in the city they could fall victim to temptation as easily as they could realize their cherished ambitions.

Paralleling the contrast of country and city was a fifth theme in Alger's juveniles, the Old versus the New World. Just as he associated corruption with urban squalor and virtue with the rural village, Alger associated social rigidity with the Old World and mobility with the New. He contended that "thousands of men" such as Lincoln "have risen to eminence in this country" after an impoverished childhood. "In England," however, "the path of promotion is more difficult, and I doubt whether any one circumstanced as Abraham Lincoln was could ever have reached a commanding position" (BacB, 78). Compared with the cultured European, Alger's caricatured, upwardly mobile American, like Henry James's Christopher Newman, is "rough and unpolished in his manners" and has "peculiar ways of regarding everything foreign to his own experience," though he is crudely attractive (BBA, 228, 238). Faintly echoing Washington Irving's observation that Europe "is rich in the accumulated treasures of age," Alger also suggested that Europe "is rich in historical associations" even though "it is a poor place to make money" (YAd, 171).

The sixth major theme in Alger's juveniles may be labeled the Search for an Identity. Each of Alger's novels for boys, unlike his fiction for adults, is a story about a hero's initiation to "self-reliance" or adult "independence" with the standard symbols of clothes, watch, and money merely denoting stages in his maturation. Frequently Alger adapted his version of the country boy myth to this initiation theme, as in *Ben the Luggage Boy* (1870) in which the hero is transformed "from a country boy of ten, to a self-reliant and independent street boy of sixteen" (BLB, 152). In all instances, the hero professes a desire to be free of dependence on a manipulative squire or stepmother. In *Luck and Pluck* (1869), for example, the hero protests that if his widowed stepmother "intends me to feel dependent, and breaks up all my plans, I will go to work for myself, and make my own way in the world" (L&P, 261). In other words, money is the crucial key to the hero's initiation because it allows him to wield adult responsibility.

Moreover, Alger developed this Search for an Identity at a more literal level than symbolic initiation. As he wrote in one novel, "Names are important" (JPB, 467), and he illustrated this idea in two ways. First, with so many orphaned heroes populating his books, he often used names to mark their search for self-awareness. The evolution of Ragged Dick into Dick Hunter and finally into Richard Hunter, Esq., and the magical transformation of the poorhouse boy Jed into Sir Robert Fenwick, Bart., explicitly signal the success of their quests for self-discovery. Alger also depicted similar, though less obviously successful quests. In *Hector's Inheritance* (1883) the hero must discover whether he deserves his classical Greek name: "Was he not Hector Roscoe after all? Had he been all his life under a mistake? If this story were true, who was he, who were his parents, what was his name?" (HI, 23). Secondly, Alger sometimes illustrated the importance of names by indicting the criminal use of an alias. "Generally, only criminals who are engaged in breaking the laws change their names," he explained

(AG, 141), and in *Paul the Peddler* (1871) he lamented the self-deception practiced by a confidence man and wife who prey "upon the community in a variety of characters" (PP, 154). These characters exist as symbolic ciphers in Alger's world, deprived even of a name by which the author could refer to them. Like Iago, whom the con-man quotes at one point, they protest that names are not important as they plot to ruin another's reputation. The hero, however, has "a natural preference for his own appellation" (HH, 192). Protective of his "good reputation and the possession of an honorable name" (ErB, 210), he refuses "to pass under an assumed name" for it would seem to him "like sailing under false colors" (St&Su, 11).

IV *Alger's Theory of Human Nature*

Although Alger did not systematically discuss in print his ideas about human nature, he did imply a theory through dozens of his juvenile books. Fundamentally, he believed—as did other Harvard Unitarians—that self-interest was both a universal human trait and, properly construed, a desirable one. As Daniel W. Howe explains, the Unitarians generally believed that "Self-love was not sinful per se. . . . It was entirely possible for the same action to be prompted both by self-love and by conscience, although if the selfish motivation became excessive, conscience would withdraw its approval."[14] Endorsing this doctrine, Alger also believed that "every man is selfish to a certain extent" (RS, 162) and that "human nature is everywhere the same. Money and rank don't change it" (SH, 79). Rightly considered, self-interest could motivate acts of charity and other practical projects. When asked why he opens his home to the hero and his family, for example, the patron in *The Tin Box* (1882) explains that "I'm a selfish old man, looking out for what will make my home happy" (TinB, 253). The hero's father in *Helping Himself* (1884–85) expresses his gratitude for "a son who, in helping himself, has been alive to help others" (HH, 245). With this theory of human nature, Alger could easily justify the political ambitions of the heroes of his biographies, as he did in Lincoln's case: "If it is said that Abraham Lincoln preferred Abraham Lincoln to any one else in the pursuit of his ambitions, and that, because of this, he was a selfish man, then I can see no objections to such an idea" (BacB, 295). Had the Great Emancipator not been ambitious to rise in politics, so the argument goes, slavery might not have been abolished when it was.

According to Alger, self-interest should also prompt employers to pay their workers well, for liberal wages would prod employees to work "with much more cheerfulness" and greater productivity (PP, 34; TomB, 257).

Like other Unitarians, Alger rejected the Calvinist doctrine of innate depravity and accepted the Arminian beliefs in individual freedom and accountability. In his juvenile novel *In a New World* (1885–86) the hero engages in a spirited debate with a villain who claims he was "fated to be" a highwayman; uneasy with this dogma, the hero proclaims that "I shouldn't like to believe as you do" (INW, 88-89). Although he accepted the Arminian faith in free will, Alger also believed in the inscrutable providence of God who allows evil to exist "for some wise purpose" ($500,164), who can shape events "to bring good out of evil" (RCS, 108), and who occasionally intercedes directly on behalf of the righteous in the affairs of this world. The hero of *In a New World*, though repelled by the doctrine of fate, places his "confidence and trust in an Overruling Power" and believes that "God had watched over him, and delivered him from danger and the schemes of wicked men" (INW, 253). The apparent contradiction in Alger's thought loses significance, however, in light of Howe's conclusion that the antebellum Harvard moralists who instructed Alger were content simply "to accept the freedom of the will as a datum of consciousness, that is, as a principle of common sense" instead of attempting to resolve the same contradiction in their own thought.[15] "Nature was kind," Alger believed (BBA, 139), and his faith in the benevolence of Nature led him to endorse doctrines of both free will and the providence of God, for each promised the eventual realization of greater human happiness on earth.

If Alger, with this elevated conception of human nature, seems to second Jefferson's claim in the Declaration of Independence that Nature has endowed all men with inalienable rights, it is because Alger also espoused a natural rights philosophy. Typically, an Alger hero possesses a natural sense of justice which entitles him "to resist any encroachment upon his rights" (BLB, 96) and to claim "the right of ordinary humanity" to defend others' rights (BB, 77). Chief among the natural rights defended by Alger and the other Harvard Unitarians was the right to hold property. The sanctity of private property is not questioned in Alger's fiction; indeed, several of his juveniles, including *Frank and Fearless* (1885), describe a hero's struggle to reclaim property his by birthright. Such a hero, according to Alger, is "not excessively fond of money" but simply will not allow himself "to be deprived of his rights" (Fr&F, 92). The thematic thrust of these novels is not in the direction of the hero's wealth-getting, but his initiation to adult independence.

Similarly, in other books Alger acknowledged the natural right of revolution. While his heroes with their natural sense of justice always submit willingly to proper authority, they rebel against tyranny. Alger's most extended defense of natural rights, including the right to oppose tyrannical authority, appears in his juvenile novel *In Search of Treasure* (1894). The son of a Massachusetts minister and Harvard graduate, the hero, Guy Fenwick, is sent by his patron to investigate allegations that the headmaster of a boarding school is "a brute and a tyrant" (IST, 80). He discovers soon after his arrival at the school, which "ought to have been a paradise" (IST, 80), that the headmaster "had been accustomed to move among his pupils like an Eastern despot, with no one bold enough to oppose him" (IST, 124). Guy, with the assistance of his patron, an Englishman named Locke (!), sparks a rebellion among the students that eventually results in the headmaster's dismissal. This school episode foreshadows another, longer episode aboard a ship whose captain, like the one in Richard Henry Dana's *Two Years Before the Mast*, is "despotic and tyrannical" (IST, 280). As Alger observed, "A captain at sea is such an autocrat that he often takes indefensible liberties, and transcends his rightful authority" (IST, 220). On one occasion this cruel captain brutally kicks a cabin boy who lies on the deck prostrate with fever. In his dealings with this English aristocrat who disdains "to meet common men on an equality" (IST, 200), Guy is urged to "stick up for your rights" (IST, 198). He resolves to be firm because "I have too much respect for myself as an American citizen to allow" civil violations (IST, 202). After Guy is marooned by the captain, the sailors nearly mutiny, the captain is murdered by an outraged sailor, and the first mate corrects the injustices upon assuming command. Alger conveniently avoided the knotty legal problem posed by the captain's death by having his murderer commit suicide. As he noted, this "self-punishment was the speediest settlement of a troublesome complication" (IST, 282).

The problem Alger addressed in such fictional situations as this was the same one James Fenimore Cooper addressed in both the Leatherstocking tales and the Littlepage series. Alger and Cooper believed that civil law ought to correspond as nearly as possible to natural law. Both authors recognized that, unfortunately, too often civil law "upholds a great deal that is oppressive and cruel," as Alger wrote (StB, 57). Not only was the law used to advance private interests, but occasionally it was used to convict the innocent (cf. ETB, 44; NYB, 221). Both Cooper and Alger advanced two solutions to the problem of the occasional discorrespondence of natural and civil law. The first was to set their fiction in the remote wilderness, far from the refining influences of civilization and outside the jurisdiction of civil law, and allow the *lex talionis* to enforce primitive justice. For example, in *Joe's Luck* (1878), set in California during the gold rush, Alger observed that "Stern was the justice which overtook the thief in those days. It was necessary, perhaps, for it was a primitive state of society, and the code which in established communities was a safeguard did not extend its protection here" (JL, 206). Their other alternative was to have characters with a natural sense of justice write, practice, and enforce the civil law. Thus it is significant that Harry Walton, the "second Franklin" of *Bound to Rise* and *Risen from the Ranks* (1873–74), enters politics; that Alger complained about the "self-sufficient and self-seeking politicians of our own day" in his biography of Webster (Farm, 228); and that, its title notwithstanding, the hero of *A Boy's Fortune* (1889) at last decides "not to go into business, but to obtain a liberal education and study law" (BF, 323). Surprisingly, perhaps, to modern readers familiar only with Alger's reputation, fifteen of his heroes become lawyers. The reason for their career selection may be read in Alger's biography of Lincoln: "When a lawyer can so bravely and affectionately rescue the innocent from the machinations of the wicked, we feel that he is indeed the exponent and representative of a noble profession. It is unfortunate that lawyers so often lend themselves to help iniquity, and oppress the weak" (BacB, 95).

Not only does the Alger hero vigorously defend his own rights, but he actively protects the rights of the weak and oppressed. The assertion that Alger "went beyond [John] Fiske and [Edward] Youmans and [William Graham] Sumner" in his social Darwinism[16] is a canard. On the contrary, Alger was neither a biological nor a social Darwinist. He believed that, instead of competing, "we all ought to help each other" (MMB, 239). Against assertions of the prerogatives of strength, he held that it is the obligation of the powerful to protect the weak. His heroes, whose "sympathies were always in favor of the oppressed" (PF, 296), always side "with the weaker against the stronger" (TTC, 62). Nor did Alger accept the Sumnerian argument, a favorite one with such plutocrats as Rockefeller and Carnegie, that wealth accumulates in the hands of the wealthy because they have been naturally selected as the fittest. "It isn't the strongest men that earn the most," Alger confided to his readers (Sl&S, 8; TTr, 62).

Although he did not interpret evolution in Darwinian terms, Alger did admit the inevitability of progress and supported his evolutionary optimism with a biological theory. Instead of explaining improvements as a "survival of the fittest," however, he explained them in terms of Lamarck's theory that mental as well as physical characteristics could be inherited. Over several generations, according to this theory, the transmission of acquired characteristics would result in progressively greater intellectual powers and moral vigor. As Alger noted in *Jack's Ward* (1875), "it requires several generations of refined habits and exemption from the coarser burdens of life to produce" more perfect people (JW, 214). Alger often traced both his hero's virtues and his snob's ugly traits to their respective parents. In *Frank and Fearless* (1885), for example, the hero's father observes that "Jasper is an improvement on the parent stock. I see in him more manliness and self-reliance than I possessed at his age" (Fr&F, 58). The feckless snob in *Tom the Bootblack* (1873), on the other hand, "inherited his father's bad traits, his selfishness and unscrupulousness, in addition to a spirit of deceitfulness and hypocrisy from his mother's nature" (TomB, 190). Both heroes and snobs in Alger's stories, in short, inherit moral characteristics of their parents.

This biological theory influenced Alger's juvenile fiction in slightly different ways during three periods of his career. It enabled him in his early juvenile novels of reform to defend self-improvement, for he believed that the acquisition and transmission of virtue were steps vital to the elevation of the species. (Alger's early juveniles will be discussed as reform documents later in this chapter.) Later, Lamarck's theory allowed Alger, especially in several books written during the 1880s and early 1890s, to stereotype racial and ethnic characters, despite his oft-repeated profession of racial and ethnic toleration. Believing that acquired characteristics could be genetically transmitted, Alger simply made the additional assumption during this period that behavior popularly attributed to some racial and ethnic groups had been so acquired. Thus Scots are depicted as reliable friends and allies, "the red man is quick to take offense, and is revengeful by nature" (Jul, 110), the Chinese "shrink from violence" (BN, 141), the Irish are "warm-hearted" (CUB, 84), and Italians are as vengeful as Indians (IST, 224). Despite Alger's profession of sympathy for the black race, he often employed the racial stereotype of the happy, superstitious darky in his books of the period, especially in *Bob Burton* (1886). And despite Alger's tutelage of the Seligman and Cardozo children, the only Jewish characters in his fiction are usurious money-lenders, modeled upon Shakespeare's Shylock, such as Joshua Starr in *Andy Gordon* (1881), Job Green in *Frank Hunter's Peril* (1885–86), and Aaron Wolverton in *Bob Burton*.

Finally, Lamarck's theory of development allowed Alger late in his life to flirt with a kind of hereditary determinism like that popular a few years later during the eugenics craze of the Progressive period. Although this seems incompatible with Alger's belief in upward mobility, it is an inconsistency analogous to his simultaneous endorsement of both free will and Providence. Alger's heroes still *choose* to be good and deserve prosperity, even as Providence or hereditary determinism selects them to be good and prosperous. These heroes always are natural aristocrats, and in his later juvenile novels Alger simply provided them with parents and sometimes grandparents whose acquired virtue the heroes have inherited. The best examples of this hereditary determinism appear in novels in which the hero, having been orphaned as a child and raised in a degrading environment, still displays "instinctive good breeding" in manners and appearance. The hero himself instinctively recognizes the difference between him and others, as in *Tom Brace* (1889): "Jack and I belong to different worlds. Though we have lived together so long, he is repulsive to me" (TBr, 33). Other characters in these novels also recognize the hero's pedigree. For example, the hero of *The Young Circus Rider* (1883) "was sometimes called 'the little gentleman' and was generally supposed to have sprung from a good family, though even to himself his birth was a secret" (YCR, 162). The mystery of how such a virtuous boy could be raised in low circumstances is solved by the eventual revelation of his noble birth. His innate virtue has been transmitted through the blood and endured years of degradation. When finally restored to his family, this hero is "drawn in almost instinctive affection" to them (JPB, 563).

Alger also applied the pseudosciences of phrenology and physiognomy to distinguish between good and evil characters in his fiction. As Russel Nye explains, phrenologists believed that the shape of the skull revealed "the shape of the brain, which in turn indicated the development of the faculties of the mind within the brain." To read a patient's character, a phrenologist palpated the skull to determine the size of as many as forty-six "organs." In the mid-nineteenth century "almost everyone believed in phrenology, and almost everyone knew and used its terminology—Poe, Whitman, Emerson, Hawthorne, and Horace Mann, among others." Much more than a psychological system, Nye concludes, phrenology appealed to reform-minded intellectuals like Emerson and Mann because it "told a man what he was and told him how to improve himself."[17] It appealed to Alger for the same reasons. A professional phrenologist in *Wait and Hope* (1877), for example, contends that "A phrenologist is never mistaken in character. Nature has stamped her impress upon each one of us, and declares unmistakably what we are." As if to ratify his testimony, he demonstrates his skill by reading the hero's skull and accurately describing his traits:

This lad has an excellent head. All the organs are well-balanced, none being in great excess. His temperament is nervous-sanguine. Hope predominates with him. He will not be easily discouraged, but when he has an object in view he will pursue it perseveringly to the end. He is not quarrelsome, but will not allow himself to be trodden upon. He has plenty of courage. He is not bashful, but respectful to his elders and superiors. He is conscientious, and more likely to do right than wrong. Of course he might yield to temptation, but it would have to be a powerful one. He has a fondness for pets, and will be kind to younger children. He will find no pleasure in ill-treating or tyrannizing over them. He has not much invention, and would make a poor machinist, but is likely to succeed in general business. He will probably be steady and reliable, and faithful to the interests of his employer. (W&H, 69–70)

Unheroic characters in Alger's juvenile fiction, however, do not fare as well. A character in *Wait and Win* (1884) who fails to respect his employer is said to possess a very small "organ of reverence" (W&W, 4), and the mercenary snob in *Facing the World* (1885) possesses a well-developed "organ of acquisitiveness" (FW, 33).

For the same reasons that he believed in phrenology, Alger accepted physiognomy, or the reading of faces for clues to character. Physiognomy seemed to be a matter of common sense to Alger, for whom fair features indicated a fair disposition and vice-versa. "Every man's face is to a certain extent indicative of his disposition and prevailing traits," he once wrote (RRH, 97).

Alger's carefully wrought distinction between hero and snob invites comparison with Jefferson's distinction between the natural aristocracy of talent and virtue and artificial aristocracy of birth and wealth. Indeed, Alger's distinction almost perfectly mirrors Jefferson's, as the following discussion in *Herbert Carter's Legacy* (1875) among the patron, snob James, and hero Herbert demonstrates:

"I hope you boys will grow up gentlemen," said Mr. Spencer.
"I shall, of course," said James.
"And you, Herbert?"
"I hope so," said Herbert; "but if it is necessary to be rich to be a gentleman, I am not sure about it."
"What is your idea of a gentleman, James?" asked the lawyer.
"He must be of a good family, and wear good clothes, and live nicely."
"Is that all?"
"He ought to be well educated."
"I see you name that last which I should name first. So these constitute a gentleman, in your opinion?"
"Yes, sir."
"Not always. I have known men combining all the qualifications you have mentioned, who were very far from being gentlemen, in my opinion."
"How is that, sir?" asked James, puzzled.
"They were arrogant, puffed up with an idea of their own importance, deficient in politeness."
"How well he has described James!" thought Herbert, but he was too much of a gentleman to say so. (HCL, 41–42)

This juvenile novel is thematically devoted to the contrast between "real gentlemen" and their "poor imitations" (HCL, 196), and in it Alger systematically used five touchstones—clothing, houses, and respective attitudes toward money, the British aristocracy, and the American working class—to illustrate their difference. Herbert, who wears patched pants because of his mother's poverty, endures the taunts of the snob in the opening paragraph of the novel. The snob, on the other hand, dresses "with a sort of pretentious gentility

which betrayed his innate vulgarity" (HCL, 214). Usually in Alger's
juvenile novels such dress includes a cane and white kid gloves. In
the New England village where the opening chapters are set, the
hero lives in a "small cottage, with something less than an acre of
land attached, enough upon which to raise a few vegetables. It
belonged to his mother, nominally, but was mortgaged for half its
value to Squire Leech, the father of James" (HCL, 3). The snob,
however, lives "in a large, square, white house, situated on an
eminence some way back from the street. It had bay windows on
either side of the front door, a gravel walk, bordered with flowers,
leading to the gate, a small summerhouse on the lawn, and alto-
gether was much the handsomest residence in the village. . . . No
wonder the squire and all the family held up their heads, and
regarded themselves as belonging to the aristocracy" (HCL, 59).
When both hero and snob meet by chance on the streets of New
York in a later chapter, they again contrast houses:

"We may come to live here," said James. "Of course, we shall live in a
brownstone front, uptown."
   "I live in a brick house," said Herbert, smiling.
   "Fashionable people live in brownstone fronts," said James.
   "I suppose I am not fashionable, then."
   "I should say not," said James. "The idea of a fashionable newsboy! It's
ridiculous." (HCL, 221–22)

The hero is glad he doesn't "think as much of money as James
Leech" (HCL, 18) and believes "something besides money is needed to make a gentleman" (HCL, 106). The snob, on his part, considers the hero "poor and proud" (HCL, 87). Alger thus condemned
his artificial aristocracy, as Thorstein Veblen did his leisure class,
for its "pecuniary canons of taste." His hero is a genuine republican
who appreciates the opportunity to rise to prominence in America;
his snob avers that "I should like to live in England, where they
have noblemen" if he could be one (HCL, 48). In the course of the
novel the hero grows vegetables, sells newspapers, and praises
Commodore Vanderbilt as a working boy who became a gentleman;
the snob refuses to perform any manual labor and admits that he
"shouldn't want the lower class to get rich. . . . They'd think they
were our equals" (HCL, 108). Although he most fully developed
his distinction between the natural and artificial aristocracies in this

book, Alger used the two character types as foils in all of his juveniles.

Although the characteristics of Alger's hero are similar to those of Jefferson's natural aristocrat, the two are not identical. As Howe suggests, "Not only talent and virtue, but also good manners, characterize the Harvard aristocrat. Now, while talent and virtue might be found anywhere, manners are a cultural advantage likely to accrue to the children of good families."[18] The beneficiary of cultural advantages himself, Alger tended to fear the snobbishness of the *nouveau riche* far more than the entrenched wealth of the old aristocracy. The heroes of both *Brave and Bold* (1872) and *Tom Tracy* (1887) court girls who belong to the First Families, and the patrons in both *Digging for Gold* (1891) and *Jed the Poorhouse Boy* (1892) have inherited their wealth rather than earned it. In *Driven from Home* (1889) Alger even offered the character of a British lord as "a model of aristocratic beauty" (DfH, 216). The snobs, significantly enough, are usually members of newly rich families; for example, James Leech, the hero's nemesis in *Herbert Carter's Legacy*, ignores the fact "that his grandfather had once been a poor mechanic. . . . He chose to consider that he had sprung from a long line of wealthy ancestors" (HCL, 108). The difficulty unique to the new-moneyed snob, as Alger explained, is that "his temptations are greater than if . . . he were born to poverty" like the hero (DofH, 33). Another newly rich character in *Tom the Bootblack* (1873) complains that his inheritance of a hundred thousand dollars "took away my ambition and energy. . . . For two years . . . I have wasted my time in drinking among unworthy companions" (TomB, 105). In a brief debate between a snob and hero in *Mark Manning's Mission* (1894) Alger revealed by inference his own aristocratic pretension:

"You must admit . . . that refinement and wealth are likely to go together. You are not too democratic for that?"
"I am not so sure. I have known many rich people who were very far from being refined." (MMM, 259)

The hero nowhere suggests, however, that refinement and poverty could go together. Alger seemed actually to fear the cultural consequences of rapid mobility and new money. Perhaps for this reason he always abandoned his hero on the threshold of his good fortune, at the cultural boundary delimiting his place, rather than following him into that strange new world of opulence; and perhaps because of the incongruity of his hero's impoverished boyhood and genteel refinement, Alger eventually attributed to his hero the "instincts of a gentleman" inasmuch as the logic of environmental conditioning which he had accepted offered him no other explanation for his gentility.

V   *Instinct and Conscience*

Of course, all of Alger's virtuous characters, even those formed from common clay, possess admirable instincts. Alger accepted the self-evident truth of the argument that, because Nature is benevolent, the instincts with which people are endowed by Nature are good. He believed that "Natural instincts" are "healthful" and "often a safer guide than reason" (Sl&S, 81; CB, 160). But sound natural instincts also require cultivation to prosper into virtues. In other words, Alger believed that virtue is not innate, although the individual with healthful instincts possesses an important incentive to virtue.

The most important natural instincts possessed by his characters are honesty, piety, neatness, kindness, and workmanship—each one a middle-class virtue in embryo. Alger's model characters, first, are honest by inclination. Although Ragged Dick had received no "religious and moral instructions . . . something told him that it was mean to steal, and he was true to this instinctive feeling" (F&F, 105). The hero of *The Young Adventurer* (1878) "was honest not so much because he had been taught that honesty was a virtue as by temperament and instinct" (YAd, 149). Occasionally, as in *Ben the Luggage Boy* (1870), a character who instinctively knows that it is wrong to steal nevertheless succumbs to temptation; he experiences an immediate sensation of guilt and, as Alger noted, requires additional instruction to realize virtue (BLB, 84).

Secondly, Alger's virtuous characters possess a natural bent to piety which is allied to their native honesty. A boy in *Phil the Fiddler* (1872), for example, is unable "to tell a falsehood" because he has "a religious nature" (PF, 355). Similarly, Ragged Dick, who unfortunately "had lived without a knowledge of God and of religious things" while a street Arab, is "not naturally irreligious." When Fosdick volunteers to teach him to pray, he is "willing to follow his example in what something told him was right" (RD, 140–

41). The hero in *Luck and Pluck* (1869) also has "a religious nature" that is trained, in this case, "in the Sunday-school" (L&P, 26).

Thirdly, believing that "perfect neatness was one of the first characteristics of a gentleman" (TelB, 63), Alger invested his virtuous characters with this instinct. These characters, even if poor, live in neat and well furnished houses or apartments, and they usually are fastidiously neat in dress, even if their clothing is frayed. In *Rough and Ready* (1869) the newsboy hero's "whole suit, though coarse, was whole, and not soiled, for he paid greater attention to dress than most boys in his line of business. This was due partly to a natural instinct of neatness, but partly also to the training he had received from his mother, who had been a neat woman" (Ro&R, 255). In this example, again, an instinct requires proper nurturing before it matures into a full-grown virtue.

Alger also invested his virtuous characters with a fourth natural capacity, the instinct of kindness. These characters most often demonstrate this instinct to be kind by preventing wife- or child-beating or cruelty to animals. Intemperate husbands and fathers molest their families with alarming regularity in such novels as *Rufus and Rose* (1870) and *Slow and Sure* (1872), and friendly neighbors or policemen are prompted to intervene on their behalf. Similarly, the hero of *Bernard Brooks' Adventures* (1893), whose "soul revolted at cruelty in any form," declares that "It will always be my business to protect children and animals from being abused" (BBA, 15). Even the young Lincoln, according to Alger's biography, composed his first essay in school on the subject of cruelty to animals, and Alger believed that Lincoln's example of kindness could influence his readers to nurture their own instinct for it. He charged them to "Emulate that tenderness of heart which led him to sympathize with 'the meanest thing that breathes,' and, like him, you will win the respect and attachment of the best men and women!" (BacB, 98).

The fifth major natural trait of Alger's virtuous characters is their instinct of workmanship—which, according to Thorstein Veblen later—"disposes men to look with favour upon productive efficiency and on whatever is of human use."[19] Alger's sympathetic characters never retire to the leisure class. If they struggle upward from penury, they acknowledge that they "should not feel happy" if they were idle and living on accumulated wealth (Sl&S, 64; LW, 69). If they are born to wealth, they contend that "the happiest men are

those who are usefully employed. Don't forget that, and never sigh
for the opportunity to lead an idle life" (TTC, 128; D&D, 34). As
Alger concluded, "It is by no means a piece of good luck to be able
to live without work. It takes away, in many cases, the healthy
stimulus to action and leaves life wearisome and monotonous. More
than one young man has been ruined by what the world called his
good fortune" (AG, 76).

The natural instinct of workmanship, as Alger formulated the
idea, is both innate—as is suggested by his analogy of his hero and
a worker-bee—and God-ordained. He frequently quoted with approval St. Paul's injunction to the Corinthians that whoever didn't
work would not eat. His faith in the efficacy of labor as a spiritual
ordinance led him to affirm the old Protestant doctrine of the Christian calling; for, as Ragged Dick's patron counsels in words similar
to those that Alger put into the mouths of virtuous characters in
dozens of his novels, "All labor is respectable, my lad, and you have
no cause to be ashamed of any honest business; yet when you can
get something to do that promises better for your future prospects,
I advise you to do so. Till then earn your living in the way you are
accustomed to, avoid extravagance, and save up a little money if
you can" (RD, 109). Alger also contended that a trade and a mercantile career are equally honorable (St&St, 348).

A character in these books can be truly satisfied only by money
he or she has earned at any useful endeavor. When a hero is offered
a job at a salary he considers excessive, a frequent occurrence in
this sentimental world, he invariably protests his overpayment. For
example, at the conclusion of Ragged Dick (1867), when the hero
is offered a job paying ten dollars a week, he truthfully admits to
his prospective employer that "It's more than I can earn" (RD, 214).
Moreover, no character in these books can derive true satisfaction
from money gained by theft, idle speculation, or beggary; as notes
the patron in Do and Dare (1882), "Even if a man could steal enough
to live upon, and were sure not to be found out, he would not enjoy
his ill-gotten gain, as an honest man enjoys the money he works
hard for" (D&D, 90). Even though he set several of his novels, such
as Joe's Luck (1878) and Ben's Nugget (1882), in the West during
the gold rush and had the hero win his good fortune through a lucky
strike, Alger distrusted such mechanisms for elevating his status.
"In my own experience," he observed in 1883, much as Thoreau
had in "Life Without Principle,"

I have known many who have been willing to move anywhere, and make any change, for the chance of earning a living more easily. About thirty years ago, a great wave of emigration flowed toward the far Pacific, and men of all callings and professions, including not a few college graduates, put on the miner's humble garb and delved for gold among the mountains and by the river-courses of California. Some came back rich, but in many cases had they been willing to work as hard and live as frugally at the East, they would have fared as well. (BacB, 144–45)

Luck was a handy—and a notoriously overworked—plot device for Alger, but he equated luck with the intercessions of an overruling Providence on behalf of the virtuous. He would have endorsed the view of one of his patrons that "What we call good luck generally comes from greater industry, good judgment, and, above all, the prompt use of opportunities" (YMin, 34). To insure that his readers would not mistake his meaning—as many recent critics have—Alger explicitly warned them that "He who trusts wholly to luck, trusts to a will-o'-the-wisp, and is about as sure of success as one who owns a castle in Spain" (ANY, 126). The instinct of workmanship, like other natural instincts, required nurturing prior to its fruition as a virtue. In almost every Alger juvenile a crisis occurs which arouses the hero's latent ambition to rise to a respectable station. In *Paul the Peddler* (1871), for example, the hero is stirred to strive when an ill friend asks him to tend his sidewalk stand for a few days.

Conscience, the moral faculty which the Unitarians viewed as the voice of God, enforces all of these benevolent impulses within virtuous men and preserves them against the temptation to succumb to the "appetites." On the one hand, conscience requires faithful cultivation of the natural, healthful instincts; for example, the hero of *Helping Himself* (1884–85) "contented himself with doing his work faithfully, and so satisfying his own conscience" (HH, 87). On the other hand, in order to sin, one must violate conscience and repress natural instinct; a villain in *Adventures of a Telegraph Boy* (1886) "had no scruple about lying" because his "conscience was elastic" (ATB, 56). To have a clear conscience, then, one simply must behave in accordance with the immutable principles of right and wrong. In his biography of James Garfield, Alger commended the recently assassinated President because

He sought, first of all, to win the approval of his own conscience and his own sense of right, and then he was willing to "take the consequences," even if they were serious enough to cut short the brilliant career which he so much enjoyed.

I conceive that in this respect he was a model whom I may safely hold up for the imitation of my readers, young or old. Such men do credit to the country, and if Garfield's rule of life could be universally adopted, the country would never be in peril. A conscientious man may make mistakes of judgment, but he can never go far astray. (Canal, 279)

Although conscience might require self-sacrifice or performance of onerous duties such as military service, the Unitarians believed that good people would prosper and prevail in the long run.

Alger also accepted the orthodox Unitarian doctrine, best defended by William Ellery Channing, that the conscience requires training and exercise before it can be wholly reliable as a moral adviser. He suggested in *The Young Miner* (1879), for example, that religious systems perform the socially useful function of training the consciences of their adherents (YMin, 64). The best illustration of conscience-training in Alger's work appears in two volumes he published in the mid-1870s—*The Young Outlaw* (1875) and its sequel, *Sam's Chance* (1876). Sam Barker, the protagonist of these novels, is, except in the final pages of the second book, an Alger anti-hero who has "no 'conceptions of duty,' or, more properly, his conscience was not very active" (YO, 28). Raised by an intemperate father, Sam simply ignores conventional morality as he smokes, gambles, and steals. Alger noted, in an authorial intrusion into the narrative, "I am afraid he is acting in a manner very unlike the well-behaved heroes of most juvenile stories, my own among the number" (YO, 74). Alger employed *in medias res* in the first of these novels, flashing back to Sam's adoption by bumbling Deacon Hopkins. On his farm the deacon has endeavored to correct Sam's deficient religious training by teaching him catechism in a scene that smacks of *Tom Sawyer*, which was published a year later:

"What's the good of the catechism?" exclaimed the deacon, shocked. "It'll l'arn you your duties. It'll benefit your immortal soul."

"I don't care if it will," said Sam, perversely. "What do I care about my soul? It never did me no good." (YO, 20)

To avoid working the Hopkins's farm, Sam steals ten dollars from the deacon and succumbs to the temptation to escape to sinful New York, that "brilliant paradise which so dazzled his youthful fancy"

(YO, 69). Unfortunately, as Alger noted, "His conscience had never been awakened to the iniquity of theft. So when it occurred to him that he had in his possession money enough to gratify his secret desire, and carry him to New York. . . . it did not occur to him that it would be morally wrong to do so" (YO, 72). On the streets of New York, Sam meets a man who invites him to his seedy apartment and filches his money. "It did not occur to him that the deacon, from whom the money was originally taken," had been similarly wronged by Sam, observed Alger. "As I have said, Sam's conscience was not sensitive, and self-interest blinded him to the character of his own conduct" (YO, 147). To survive in these hostile surroundings Sam attempts several brief deviations from normal behavior. At first, he begs or steals food. Then, in quick succession, he blacks boots for another boy until he is dismissed for cheating on receipts; blatantly lies to the superintendent of the Newsboys' Lodging House in order to live there; and finally secures steady employment until, tempted by a friend, he absconds with some funds belonging to his employer and plays billiards. Again he is dismissed. Unemployed and hungry, he returns a lost child to his home and is rewarded by the grateful parents with a meal, a gift of five dollars, and "the post of errand boy at five dollars a week" (YO, 246). His essential reward, however, is not money but an invitation "to fill an humble but respectable position in life" (YO, 246).

The sequel chronicles Sam's gradual reformation through the refining influence of his roommate, a conscientious office boy. While Sam continues to live profligately, wasting time and money on idle amusement each evening and borrowing clothes and money when his week's salary is exhausted, his friend and foil Henry Martin lives frugally, studying at night and carefully husbanding his weekly salary of five dollars. As Alger noted, Henry "had begun to think of the future, and to provide for it. This is always an encouraging sign, and an augury of success. Sam had not got so far yet" (SC, 34). Both Sam and Henry invest small amounts of their earnings in hopes of realizing a dividend—Sam in a Cuban lottery ticket and Henry, who borrows capital on the security of his bank passbook, in a shipment of goods to Rotterdam underwritten by his employer. Of course, Sam's "golden dreams of fortune" (SC, 100) are dashed, while Henry reaps a windfall of a hundred dollars. At length, Sam steals his roommate's savings book, though he "blushed with shame" in the act of theft (SC, 114). As if receiving a just punishment, he soon is discharged from his job for gross negligence and then is

confronted by Henry with the evidence of his theft. The latter
incident in particular stirs Sam's long-stilled conscience. Suddenly,
"The enormity of his act flashed upon him" (SC, 139) as it had not
after his theft from Deacon Hopkins in the first volume. When he
realizes that he could carry the stigma of dishonor for the rest of
his life, there is "kindled in him a new and honorable ambition to
attain a respectable position in society." In other words, "Sam's
conscience had become more sensitive than formerly" (SC, 189).
Eventually, he is urged by some college students he meets to "lay
aside all your bad habits, and try to become refined and gentle-
manly" (SC, 234). In a contrived conclusion to the novel, he is hired
at a liberal salary to serve as a companion to a crippled boy, is
admitted to membership in his family, and repairs his broken friendship with Henry. Still, in its entirety the novel demonstrates that
his awakened conscience has been rigorously exercised.

VI *The Importance of Good Habits*

Although late in his career Alger seemed increasingly to espouse
a kind of genetic determinism, in his early juvenile fiction especially
he hewed to the orthodox Unitarian line. As Howe explains, "To
the Unitarian humanist, the doctrine of perfectibility was the foundation of all efforts to aid the poor." Joseph Tuckerman, for example,
believed "that a Calvinist preacher who went into the slums teaching
predestination and depravity did more harm than good." Moreover,
"the obstacles that Unitarian moralists conceived to stand in the
way of the moral progress of the poor were environmental, not
hereditary."[20] In his early juvenile reform novels, those written
mainly before 1880, Alger was clearly an environmentalist, as is
evinced by his faith in the refining influences of civilization and his
appeals for the cultivation of natural instincts and training of the
conscience. Occasionally he was even more explicit in discussing
the influence of environment on the building of character. In *Slow
and Sure* (1872) he stated his rationale for benevolence: "Our des-
tinies are decided more than we know by circumstances. If the
street boys, brought up to a familiarity with poverty, and often with
vice and crime, go astray, we should pity as well as condemn, and
if we have it in our power to make the conditions of life more
favorable for any, it is our duty, as the stewards of our common

Father, to do what we can" (Sl&S, 119). In short, in his early juveniles Alger suggested that right influences *alone* were necessary to reform the poor. Only later did he begin skeptically to admit that "It is not always easy to say what circumstances have most influence in shaping the destiny of a boy" (Canal, 48) and to qualify his earlier facile optimism.

Environment was crucial to the shaping of character, in the orthodox Unitarian view, because of its role in the formation of good or bad habits. As Howe observes, their "goal was to make the performance of duty so routine, through the cultivation of good habits, that virtue would become automatic."[21] Or as Dugald Stewart advised in one of Alger's Harvard texts, "To habituate the minds of children to those occupations and enjoyments alone, which it is in the power of an individual, at all times, to command, is the same solid foundation that can be laid for their future tranquillity."[22] For this reason, Alger urged his young readers to develop good habits and to resist the temptation to form bad ones.

The habits he most frequently recommended were saving money, studying, and attending church. Francis Bowen, one of Alger's Harvard instructors, was also one of the first Unitarians to conclude, on the basis of anthropological research, that a disposition to save money was not an innate but an acquired trait.[23] Like other Unitarian moralists, Alger's concern with the habit of wise economy was not purely economic, however. As he noted, "Of greater value than the sum" accumulated "was the habit of self-denial and saving which our hero had formed" (RfR, 141). The habit of saving thus became a strong recommendation of a character's trustworthiness to adult landlords and employers. In *Fame and Fortune* (1868), an adult tells the hero, "Boys who have formed so good a habit of saving can be depended upon" (Fa&F, 11). In these novels heroes often open bank accounts or carefully set aside a part of their weekly earnings. Alger's plan in describing these routine deposits, however, was not to titillate his readers with the sound of cash registers, but to depict a good habit which entitles the hero to good fortune and to encourage his readers to imitate such thrift. In *Mark the Match Boy* (1869) Alger even explained an arrangement in the Newsboys' Lodging House which encouraged boys to deposit money for safekeeping with the superintendent. This arrangement, according to Alger, had a tendency to teach frugal habits to the young patrons of the Lodge. Extravagance is one of their besetting sins. Many average a dollar and over as daily earnings, yet are always ragged and out at elbows, and often are unsupplied with the small price of a night's lodging at the Home. The money is squandered on gambling, cigars, and theatre-going, while the same sum would make them comfortable and independent of charity. The disposition to save is generally the first encouraging symptom in a street boy, and shows that he has really a desire to rise above his circumstances, and gain a respectable position in the world. (MMB, 293)

By offering the street boys an alternative to squalid conditions and the opportunity to form good habits, the Lodge justified its existence as a benevolent institution.

A second habit Alger hoped his young readers would form was regular study or self-cultivation. A fuller discussion of Alger's thoughts on education appears later in this chapter; however, it may be briefly noted here that he favored the habit of study, as he did the habit of saving, because of the merit of self-culture, not because it might lead to financial profit. While still a bootblack, for example, Ragged Dick forms "the habit of spending a portion of every evening in improving reading or study" because he wanted to become respectable, "and he meant to earn it by hard study" (MMB, 223). Although the self-culture eventually does qualify him for better employment at a higher salary, "Dick had gained something more valuable than money" with his habit, as Alger was careful to explain (RD, 167).

A third habit Alger recommended to his readers was regular church-going. Because he believed that religious systems were instrumental in the training of their adherents' consciences, his primary concern with this habit again was morality rather than status. In addition to the habits of saving and studying, Dick forms the habit of church attendance. He begins to attend a church regularly because he wishes to become respectable, and only two years later is asked to become a Sunday school teacher. The virtuous poor in these books, who are understandably reluctant to attend church "for want of good clothing, not for any want of respect for religious institutions," often enroll in a church immediately after obtaining a modest income, as in *Slow and Sure* (1872): "Mrs. Hoffman felt glad once more to find herself enjoying religious privileges, and determined henceforth to attend regularly" (Sl&S, 72).

Alger and other Unitarians believed that the formation of good habits while young would tend to prevent the adoption of more vicious patterns of behavior later in life. Conversely, once a child had adopted bad habits, they thought, it would be nearly impossible to convert that person to the straight and narrow path of clean living. At the conclusion of *Ben the Luggage Boy* (1870), for example, Alger noted that the hero is only "gradually laying aside the injurious habits which he acquired in his street life" (BLB, 289). As a consequence, in his juvenile fiction Alger condemned the formation of bad habits much more often and explicitly than he commended the formation of good ones, and even after he had begun to doubt the efficacy of good habits alone as a stimulus to reform he persisted in portraying the baneful effects of bad ones. For this reason, his later novels tend to contain long passages of tiresome didacticism.

Alger also presented in his juvenile fiction a greater variety of bad than good habits. Many of them warrant only a passing warning, such as his admonitions against the habitual use of coffee, drugs, and profanity. The habit of billiard-playing, while not technically bad (Alger himself occasionally indulged in a game), still received his frequent censure for "paving the way to intemperance," indolence, and gambling, "as bars are generally connected with such establishments" (HI, 221). He reserved his most strident condemnations for the habits of drinking, smoking, and gambling. Active in the temperance crusade as a minister, Alger continued to preach in his fiction against the "pernicious habit" of drinking (TBr, 17). Indeed, he recurrently described intemperate behavior as a sin (LW, 62; FW, 95), and well over half of his juvenile books contain a warning to his young readers to beware of Demon Rum. Perhaps the best example appears in *Rough and Ready* (1869): "In a great city like New York, there are many men . . . who, for the brief pleasure of the intoxicating cup, throw away their own happiness and welfare, and spoil the happiness of others. Think of this picture, boy-reader, and resolve thus early that such a description shall never apply to you!" (Ro&R, 69–70). In general, Alger condemned intemperate habits for the two reasons suggested by this admonition. First, he considered alcoholism a "sin against health" (FW, 95), not an illness. He believed that alcoholics were basically weak-willed souls who became "slaves to their appetites" (YAd, 179) in deliberate violation of their consciences. The second reason Alger condemned intemperance was a social one—he believed it robbed the drinker of respectability, sometimes wealth, position, or family, and happiness. For example, a once-prosperous lawyer in *A Cousin's Conspiracy* (1896) unfortunately "had succumbed to the love of drink and gradually lost his clients and his position" (CC, 119). Because of the physical and social damage caused by intemperance Alger proposed to remove the temptation to form this habit. Not only did he repeatedly discourage his readers from taking their first drink, but he insistently endorsed the benevolent work of temperance societies, which he believed "exert a good influence" (YMus, 209).

In about half of his juvenile books Alger also admonished his readers to avoid the habit of smoking, and his two reasons for doing so closely paralleled his criticisms of drinking. As one of his heroes outlines them, "There is no danger of my smoking. I don't think it would do me any good. Besides, it is expensive" (RfR, 7). Smoking, like drinking, jeopardizes health and costs too much money. In *Mark the Match Boy* (1869) Alger explained the health risk to the user of tobacco in a passage that also evinces his environmental bias: "Not naturally bad, [improvident boys] drift into bad habits from the force of outward circumstances. They early learn to smoke or chew, finding in tobacco some comfort during the cold and wet days, either ignorant of or indifferent to the harm which the insidious weed will do to their constitution. So their growth is checked, or their blood is impoverished, as is shown by their pale faces" (MMB, 256). No young boy, Alger believed, "can smoke without being affected injuriously. Men are frequently injured by smoking, and boys always" (RD, 43). Still, the more persuasive reason to abstain from smoking, as he admitted, was economic. The frugal hero in *Ben the Luggage Boy* (1870) "gave up smoking,—not so much because he considered it injurious, but because cigars cost money, and he was economizing in every possible way" (BLB, 256). Unfortunately, in Alger's view, other less virtuous characters fail to break the expensive habit. Confidence men often brag about the money they conspicuously consume in smoke. In short, Alger vigorously defended what he called his "old-fashioned ideas on the subject of drinking and smoking" (W&W, 153). His observation that "in college James Garfield neither drank nor smoked" (Canal, 157) was not, as it might seem to be, a casual remark, but vital information about the model character he offered to his readers.

In nearly half of his juvenile books Alger also warned his readers about the "seductive lures of the gaming-table" (YMin, 189). Although the habit was not itself a health risk, it was expensive. Miners in Alger's Western novels often gamble away fortunes they laboriously have accumulated. Their foolish prodigality is like that of the purchasers of lottery tickets in other novels, for as one hero tells a snob, "Buying lottery tickets is about the most foolish investment you could make" (D&D, 101). Moreover, Alger tried to link causally the passion for gambling and theft; to sustain his expensive habit, the gambler in his books usually is tempted to steal. A pickpocket in *The Young Adventurer* (1878) offers the following account of his moral decay:

> Five years ago I was a favorite in society. One day an acquaintance introduced me into a gambling house, and I tried my hand successfully. I went out with fifty dollars more than I brought in. It was an unlucky success, for it made me a frequent visitor. All my surplus cash found a market there, and when that was exhausted I borrowed from my employer [without his knowledge]. For six months I evaded discovery. Then I was detected. My friends interceded and saved me from the penitentiary; but I lost my situation and was required to leave the city. I went to New York, tried to obtain a situation there, failed, and then adopted my present profession. (YAd, 141)

Even if a gambler could outwit chance and improve his fortunes, Alger opined, he would still be no better than a thief, for "money won at play must be classed among ill-gotten gains" (HH, 150). Again, money has to be earned in a creditable manner to be deserved. Thus Alger offered his readers the same advice found in the standard manuals of the self-help theorists of the period, even repeating their reasons for condemning insobriety, smoking, and gambling.

VII   *Social and Political Content of the Works*

Alger's avowed expectations for his juvenile works suffered a steady diminution. According to the author himself, his early juvenile novels served a twofold purpose: to exert a salutary influence upon the class of boys about whom he wrote by offering them moral exemplars, and to document for the public record "the life and experiences of the friendless and vagrant children who are now numbered by thousands in New York and other cities," in the hope "that the result will be to strengthen and assist the philanthropic efforts which are making to rescue them [*sic*] from their vagabond condition."[24] Alger claimed he was so successful in accomplishing the latter in the six-volume "Ragged Dick series" (1867–70) that he continued his "true histories" in the eight-volume "Tattered Tom series" (1871–79). This series included his most noteworthy social novel, *Phil the Fiddler* (1872), an exposé of the padrone system which has been called "a minor *Uncle Tom's Cabin*,"[25] and *Julius* (1874), a novel about the program of orphan resettlement administered by the Children's Aid Society. In his preface to the last of the novels in the "Tattered Tom series," *The Telegraph Boy* (1879), Alger expressed his gratitude for the favorable response accorded his work and called anew for philanthropic contributions to elevate and redeem the boys who were his subjects:

The "Telegraph Boy" completes the series of sketches of street-life in New York inaugurated eleven years since by the publication of "Ragged Dick." The author has reason to feel gratified by the warm reception accorded by the public to these pictures of humble life in the great metropolis. He is even more gratified by the assurance that his labors have awakened a philanthropic interest in the children whose struggles and privations he has endeavored faithfully to describe. He feels it his duty to state that there is no way in which these waifs can more effectually be assisted than by contributing to the funds of "The Children's Aid Society," whose wise and comprehensive plans for the benefit of their young wards have already been crowned with abundant success.[26]

Alger rarely sounded this note in his juvenile fiction again, probably because such a philanthropic concern could not be sustained among his readers. After plowing this field in fourteen "urban" novels, he apparently was compelled to write more sensational stories in order to appeal to a broader juvenile audience. His four-volume "Brave and Bold series" (1872–77) consisted of more pulpy stuff than his earlier social fiction, and the four volumes in the sensational "Pacific series" (1878–82) were only slightly more sophisticated than the dime novels he attacked in his fiction and criticism. The only social comment he could afford in these novels appeared obliquely in *Ben's Nugget* (1882), in which there appears a Chinese character "whose virtues," he hoped, would "go far to diminish the prejudice which, justly or unjustly, is now felt toward his countrymen."[27] In the four-volume "Atlantic series" (1883–85) Alger abandoned all pretense of social criticism, admitting in his preface to *The Young Circus Rider* (1883) that he was writing "stories of life and adventure" (YCR, 3). This admission, in fact, appeared in one of the last prefaces Alger prepared for publication. Though he continued for over a decade to write several novels per year, he rarely afforded himself again the luxury of public comment on them.

Alger's original commitment to a social fiction with realistic dimensions seems apparent enough. His rationale for reform was best articulated by a patron in one of his books: "Whatever talents we possess our Creator meant us to exercise for our benefit and the pleasure of the community" (DD, 156). This moral basis for reform led the mugwumpish Alger to endorse incidentally in his fiction such proposals as those for civil service, the liberalization of divorce laws, and female suffrage. Most of his interest in social reform, however, centered early around four major topics in addition to temperance: children's aid, other forms of charity and philanthropy, racial toleration, and education.

In many respects Alger's earliest juvenile novels were little more than advertisements for the reformation of children through the influence of the Children's Aid Society and the Newsboys' Lodging House. Alger best expressed his justification of children's aid and its methods in a brief passage in *Brave and Bold* (1872): "If the community, while keeping vigilant watch over the young outcasts that throng our streets, plying their petty avocations, would not always condemn, but encourage them sometimes to a better life, the results would soon appear in the diminution of the offenses for which they are most frequently arrested" (B&B, 189). Not surprisingly, in light of Alger's faith in community benevolence, nearly three dozen of his novels, most of which appeared prior to 1880, refer to the Children's Aid Society, its founder Charles Loring Brace, or the lodging houses it sponsored. Often in the prefaces to these novels Alger acknowledged his debt of inspiration to his sources, but more often the fiction itself evinces the debt. For example, Ragged Dick, who lives in the Newsboys' House, strongly recommends it to another character: "It's a good place. I don't know what us boys would do without it. They give you supper for six cents, and a bed for five cents more" (RD, 78). One entire chapter in *Mark the Match Boy* (1869) is set in the House. Deep into the narrative of *Ben the Luggage Boy* (1870) Alger interrupted his story to declare editorially, "The Lodging House, though it cannot supply the place of a private home, steps between hundreds of boys and complete vagabondage, into which, but for its existence, they would quickly lapse. Probably no money is more wisely expended than that which enables the Children's Aid Society of New York to maintain this and kindred institutions" (BLB, 117). As late as 1894, Alger described his hero adrift in New York yet paying only eighteen cents daily "for supper, a bed, and breakfast" at the Lodge (RS, 28).

Alger's strongest endorsement of children's aid appears in *Phil the Fiddler* (1872), his depiction of young Italian immigrant boys forced to beg on the streets of New York in exchange for room and board provided by an overseer to whom each is legally indentured. In this novel of strident social criticism Alger exploited the opportunity to comment sardonically on mercenary fathers: "What wonder that the boys sold into such cruel slavery should be estranged from the fathers who for a few paltry ducats sell the liberty and happiness of their children" (PF, 299). The cruel padrone to whom Filippo, or Phil, is indentured delights "in inflicting pain and anguish upon others" (PF, 309), and he even murders one of his charges. The civil law, according to Alger, had failed to preserve the natural rights of these boys: "I know of no case where the law has stepped in to rescue the young victim" (PF, 315). Aided by another character, Phil voids his legal contract of indenture and escapes across the Hudson River to New Jersey, much like a runaway slave crossing the Ohio River to the North. There he is protected by an Irish family from the padrone's efforts to capture him. Finally, he is rescued half-frozen from a snowdrift by a kindly old doctor "whose skill was so appreciated that he had already, although still in the prime of life, accumulated a handsome competence" (PF, 389). The doctor resuscitates Phil, and he and his wife ask him to remain with them as their son, replacing one of identical age who had died. "So our little hero had drifted into a snug harbor," Alger concluded. "His toils and privations were over. And for the doctor and his wife it was a glad day also. On Christmas day four years before they had lost a child. On this Christmas, God had sent them another to fill the void in their hearts" (PF, 393). Phil's reward is not fortune, but a good home.

In every juvenile book he wrote Alger praised universal philanthropy and charity, using the Golden Rule, not gold, as his standard of virtue. Indeed, Alger's faith in the efficacy of charity was so pronounced that it becomes a principle of social reform in his fiction, and each "cheerful giver" a reformer of a social order structured to reward selfishness. The pleasure of doing good becomes its own reward in Alger's Unitarian view, and he recurrently mentioned in his fiction the delight enjoyed by the charitable giver, as in *Walter Griffith* (1887): "Money never gives so much pleasure as when it is spent to make others happy" (WG, 247). Similarly, a childless millionaire in *Rough and Ready* (1869), whose "home was empty of comfort and happiness," might have corrected this, according to Alger, had he only diverted "a trifling rill, from his full stream of riches, to the channel of charity; but this never entered his mind" (Ro&R, 49). Still, Alger believed that "It is often those who have little, that are most ready to help others poorer than themselves." In this way, charity becomes an instrument of social reform, for "if everyone had a heart as warm" as his virtuous characters, "there would be little misery or suffering in the world" (MMM, 175). Each of Alger's heroes, while still poor as a churchmouse, contributes his widow's mite to aid others. In *Andy Grant's Pluck* (1895) the hero freely gives money to a poor family and rejoices in this evidence of his own virtue: "Andy felt a warm glow in his heart at the thought of the happiness he had been instrumental in bringing to the poor family. He had learned the great lesson that some never learn, that there is nothing so satisfactory as helping others. We should have a much better world if that was generally understood" (AGP, 177). Even after these heroes receive their good fortune near the end of the novels, they still exercise their charitable affections. At the close of *Mark the Match Boy* (1869) Dick has so stirred a patron by his acts of charity that the patron endows the Newsboys' Lodge with a thousand dollars, and gives Dick an additional thousand dollars "as a charity fund" so that "whenever I have an opportunity of helping along a boy who is struggling upward as I once had to struggle, I will do it." To this the patron responds, "A noble resolution, Mr. Hunter! You have found out the best use of money" (MMB, 381). In short, Alger praised acts of charity and suggested that money is best used as a means of helping others, not as an end unto itself.

Alger strongly sympathized with the poor in his books and righteously condemned the parsimonious plutocrats who infest his stories. Dugald Stewart, in the text assigned Alger's Harvard class in moral philosophy, claimed that "As the unfortunate chiefly stand in need of our assistance, so there is provided in every breast a most powerful advocate in their favour; an advocate, to whose solicitations it is impossible even for the most obdurate to turn always a deaf ear."[28] This innate sense of sympathy for the unfortunate and oppressed accounts for the willingness of the virtuous to aid the poor: "While it is a good thing to save money," Alger wrote in 1888, "it is still better to use it judiciously to aid those who stand in need of a helping hand" (NYB, 260). To deserve prosperity and the title of Christian, a character in these books must practice an active sympathy for the poor. The young lawyer Lincoln, Alger noted, was even "known at times to remit fees justly due when his client was unfortunate" (BacB, 99). Alger also revealed a sociological bent in his discussions of the plight of the poor in his novels. In *Charlie Codman's Cruise* (1866), for example, he lamented that the poor are compelled to pay more proportionally for their "scant and insufficient accommodations than the rich. . . . No class of property is made to pay a larger percentage than the wretched tenement-houses which seem adapted to furnish as little accommodation as possible to those who are compelled to occupy them" (CCC, 43). And in *The Train Boy* (1883) he raised the possibility, a generation before the publication of Upton Sinclair's *The Jungle*, that Chicago-processed minced meat, a staple in the diet of the impoverished, contained the flesh of dogs and cats (TrB, 26). Borrowing Joseph Tuckerman's distinction between poverty and pauperism, Alger indicated that there existed " a great difference between respectable and squalid poverty" (ErB, 83). Those who are respectably poor at least support themselves or deserve the help they do receive, often sharing their small bounty with others. To ease the strain on the respectable poor, Alger proposed the simple solution of private charity. He wrote in *Luke Walton* (1887–88) that

I have seen gentlemen, handsomely dressed, and evidently with plenty of money, speak roughly to these young boys. It always makes me indignant. Why should they have so easy a time, while there are so many who don't know where their next meal is coming from? Why, what such a man spends for his meals in a single day would support a poor newsboy in comfort for a week. . . . There must always be poor people, but those who are more fortunate ought at least to give them sympathy. It is the least acknowledgment they can make for their own more favored lot. (LW, 20–21)

Concerned by the legal authority of landlords to evict the poor from their tenants, Alger wrote that "A rich man who will take advantage of a poor man's necessity to deprive him of his home deserves to be horsewhipped" (YMin, 230), and he contended that charitable landlords were obligated sometimes to *reduce* their rents to ease the burdens on the poor (WBH, 280). And lest Alger suffer the accusation that he ignored the plight of the immigrant poor, it should be noted that three of his heroes—in *Phil the Fiddler* (1872), *Only an Irish Boy* (1874), and *The Young Salesman* (1894–95)—do not enjoy the advantages of native citizenship during their trials of fortune.

Neither innocent nor entirely naive, Alger acknowledged that either the giver or recipient of charity could engage in a fraud that would render the charitable act meaningless. Much as Jesus condemned public displays of charity in the Sermon on the Mount, Alger criticized flaunted philanthropy in his juvenile books. In *Try and Trust* (1871), for example, he noted that the villain contributed to the poor only if "his benevolence was likely to obtain sufficient publicity. Mr. Stanton did not believe in giving in secret. What was the use of giving money away unless you could get credit for it? That was the principle upon which he always acted" (T&T, 11). Rich men may also deliberately pretend to be philanthropists for personal advantage. The villain in *Luke Walton* (1887–88) harbors political ambitions and so carefully cultivates his public image as

a philanthropist. He was president of one charitable society and treasurer of another. At the annual meetings of these societies he was always called upon to speak, and his allusions to the poverty and privations of those who were cared for by these societies never failed to produce an impression.

"What a good man he is!" said many who listened with sympathetic interest.

It was popularly supposed that he gave away large sums in charity. Indeed, he admitted the fact, but explained the absence of his name from subscription papers by saying: "All my gifts are anonymous. Instead of giving my name, I prefer to put down 'Cash,' so much, or 'A Friend,' such another sum. I don't wish to influence others, but it jars upon me to have my name ostentatiously paraded in the public prints."

Now, in all subscriptions there are donations ascribed to "Cash" and "A Friend," and whenever these occurred, it was generally supposed they represented Mr. Browning. But, to let the reader into the secret, this was only a shrewd device of Mr. Browning's to have the reputation of a philanthropist at little or no expense, for, as a matter of fact, he never contributed at all! (LW, 113)

This mock philanthropist is just as dishonest as the recipient who exaggerates his needs, for both deprive the respectable poor of the charity they require. In *Mark Stanton* (1890) a shiftless though able-bodied woman adopts "the profession of mendicancy" and begs on the street on behalf of five children she invents for the occasion. Until she is caught in her lie by a representative of a charitable society, she succeeds with her appeals for money. After one kind but unwise woman contributes to her fraudulent cause, Alger noted, "The good lady whose charitable feelings had been so imposed upon, walked on with the pleasant consciousness that she had relieved a deserving and destitute family. It is unfortunate that there are so many impostors, who, on being found out, prevent real cases of distress from being considered" (MS, 17, 75). Like other Harvard moralists, Alger in this incident "cautioned against charity that reflected mere benevolent impulses. Giving, in order to be effective, had to be rationally disciplined, and designed to do the most good in the long run. . . . Invariably, the Unitarians' charity was intended to reform and uplift the poor, not merely to mitigate their sufferings."[29] Unless the worthiness of the appeal for money could be demonstrated, Alger, like most nineteenth-century Yankees, assumed that money alone would not benefit the recipient except temporarily. The patron in *Cast Upon the Breakers* (1893), for example, finds a job for the hero rather than simply giving him money, because she believes that when the money "was gone you would be no better off" (CUB, 128). In short, Alger thought that "the difference between the rich merchant and the ragged fellow who solicits his charity as he is stepping into his carriage, consists, frequently, not in natural ability, but in the fact that the one has used his ability as a stepping-stone to success, and the other has suffered his to become stagnant, through indolence, or dissipation" (Ro&R, 227).

The final element in Alger's defense of social reform through the influence of organized charities consists of his argument that charitable societies could act as trustees of the commonwealth and thus ought to inherit endowment funds from private bequests. Although Alger did not express in print an opinion about the landmark Supreme Court decision *Vidal et al. v. Philadelphia*—more commonly known as the Girard Will case—occasionally he seemed to allude in his fiction to this unsuccessful attempt by the relatives of the late Stephen Girard to set aside the terms of the will which left seven million dollars to found a college for poor white male orphans. Had he offered an opinion explicitly, it is likely that Alger would have favored the decision, for he consistently defended the right of private charities to inherit money willed to them over the protests of "selfish" relatives. A selfish distant cousin in *Herbert Carter's Legacy* (1875), for example, contends that the deceased "had no right to put off his own flesh and blood with a beggarly pittance, and leave all his money to the town." The honest lawyer who reads the will responds, "Pardon me; whatever you may think of Mr. Carter's will, there is no doubt that he had a perfect legal right to dispose of [his money] as he did" (HCL, 25). Alger wished to preserve and defend this legal right, and to this end he praised Webster in his biography *From Farm Boy to Senator* (1882) for successfully defending in the Dartmouth College case the legal autonomy of "every eleemosynary institution throughout our country." (In the same book he completely ignored Webster's unsuccessful arguments to undermine that autonomy in the Girard case.)

Alger shared the racial toleration common among Unitarians, and this toleration led him to espouse a third set of social reforms. His first two juvenile novels, *Frank's Campaign* (1864) and *Paul Prescott's Charge* (1865), were basically propaganda justifying the Civil War as a measure required to destroy the horrible Southern slave system. Two characters in *Frank's Campaign*, for example, reveal the fervor of his indignation about slavery. The first is a benevolent "colored woman, who until a few months since had been a slave in Virginia. Finally she had seized a favorable opportunity, and taking the only child which the cruel slave system had left her, for the rest had been sold South, succeeded in making her way into Pennsylvania" (FC, 73–74). Another is a literate slave who can converse intelligently about such uncharacteristic subjects as Shakespeare's plays, but who has been denied the freedom to develop further his genteel "acquirements" (FC, 179). Alger's willingness to excuse slave escapes, though these were violations of the civil law, was later evinced in *Phil the Fiddler* (1872) and *Bob Burton* (1886–87), a novel set in antebellum Iowa in which the hero's companion is a young fugitive slave from Arkansas. He also condemned slavery in his biography of Webster as "the one great flaw in our otherwise glorious system of government," and indeed he criticized Webster for going "too far in his concessions" by accepting the Compromise of 1850 (Farm, 273, 274). In *Bob Burton* he also lamented the racial prejudice of those who, in whatever period, consider themselves innately superior to black people. In addition to defending the natural rights of blacks in his books, Alger acknowledged that the rights of two other racial minorities, the Indians and the Chinese, had been infringed. In *Tom Thatcher's Fortune* (1882) he suggested that the responsibility for the "Indian problem" was "not wholly on their side. They have been badly treated by our race" (TTF, 172). And in *Tom Tracy* (1887) Alger's hero defends a Chinese man from the racial abuse threatened by a gang of drunken sailors. Against those who wished to restrict Chinese immigration Alger asserted the right of "all who wish to make a home" in this country (YEx, 212). He condemned in several of his juvenile novels the tactics of racial intimidation practiced by Ku Klux Klan-like vigilante groups, such as the "Knights of the Skull" in *Tom Brace* (1889) and the masked "Black Band of Boy Outlaws" in *Walter Griffith* (1887).

Alger also shared the vaulted Unitarian faith in the importance of liberal education as a tool of social reform. Around his faith clustered a fourth constellation of reform impulses. As Howe suggests, "The school was as important as the church in the eyes of the Unitarian moralists. In fact, the church and the school had essentially the same mission, for both were basically character-building institutions, guiding people in the formation of industrious habits, religious principles, and refined sentiments."[30] Himself a teacher in New England schools for several years and a private tutor for two decades after that, Alger acclaimed the social role of education in his books and often wove instruction in a variety of subjects into the fabric of his narratives. Unlike the entrepreneurs who recommended that aspiring captains of industry obtain a commercial or technical education, Alger, who had been a Phi Beta Kappa scholar at Harvard, believed that the acquisition of literally *any* form of knowledge was useful because it could spark the reformation of students and societies. In other words, education was important to Alger, first, as an ameliorating influence. As he wrote in 1884, "Any kind of knowledge is likely to prove of service" in this regard (W&W, 87). He depicted the subjects of his three juvenile biographies as scholars whose sentiments had been refined by the store of liberal knowledge they had obtained. For good reasons, Alger repeated the popular story of Lincoln as a boy learning to read borrowed books by firelight, and he suggested too that Garfield added "to his stock of general knowledge" in those "spare moments which others devoted to recreation" (Canal, 62). As he concluded in his biography of Webster, "My young readers will find that knowledge never comes amiss, but, in the course of a long and sometimes of a short life, we are generally able to employ it for our advantage" (Farm, 168). Dozens of Alger's heroes study a foreign language, often a classical language, despite the apparent impracticality of this scholarship, because of the pleasure they receive from the mental exercise. The following conversation appears in *Shifting for Himself* (1876):

". . . a good education is a good thing for any one to possess, be he rich or poor."
"You wouldn't advise a boy that was going to be a mechanic to study Latin or Greek, would you?"
"If he liked it." (SH, 39)

Knowledge is evidence of moral worth or respectability, and Alger's heroes desperately struggle to obtain it. Ragged Dick studies geography and grammar as a bootblack, and later as a clerk acquires a rudimentary knowledge of French. The hero of *The Erie Train Boy* (1890) enrolls in "evening classes of the Young Men's Christian Association" to correct the deficiencies in his education (ETB, 193). Alger even proposed that ambitious youngsters organize their own associations for mutual edification: "I heartily approve of societies organized by young people for debate and mutual improvement. They are oftentimes productive of great good. Some of our distinguished men date their first impulse to improve and advance themselves to their connection with such a society" (MMB, 352). In an era when students rarely could afford, either in time or money, the luxury of a college education Alger often had his heroes attend Ivy League schools. So pronounced was his faith in the beneficent influences of education that over a dozen of his heroes enter upon teaching careers.

Although Alger went to great lengths to suggest that "knowledge is better than land or gold" (BR, 18), he did admit that another benefit of a sound education was its marketability. No well-educated adult need fear destitution, he often asserted. He wrote that "Education often enables a man to make money" (FC, 24). A college education, though ideally obtained for reasons other than personal aggrandizement, still represented a kind of income insurance. The hero of *Walter Sherwood's Probation* (1890), when unemployed, reassures himself by posing a rhetorical question: "Did he not possess a knowledge more or less extensive of Latin, Greek and mathematics, with a smattering of French and German, not to speak of logic, rhetoric, etc.? For one of his age he considered himself quite accomplished, and he persuaded himself that the world would receive him at his own estimate. It would be very strange if he could not earn a living, when hundreds and thousands of his age, without a tithe of his knowledge, managed to live" (WSP, 72).

The greater importance of education as a socially refining influence than as a practical tool for elevating status is reflected in the types of lessons Alger coyly introduced into his books. To be sure, they often contain examples of elementary bookkeeping, math problems for readers to solve, and lessons in grammar and punctuation, but far more frequently Alger sought to instruct his readers in the more liberal branches of learning. His biographies offered him the opportunity to teach history, so in the Webster volume, for example, he discussed the intricacies of Jefferson's embargo policy. The multilingual Alger often instructed his readers in other languages, implying that their study "helps one to a knowledge of the grammar" of one's native tongue (VV, 91). Thus in *Strive and Succeed* (1872) Alger quoted in Latin and then translated for his readers the opening sentences of the second book of Caesar's *Commentaries on the Gallic War*, quoted and translated some common German sayings in *A Rolling Stone* (1894), and inserted into *The Train Boy* (1883) such French words and phrases as *parti, distingué, empressement, carte blanche*, and *recherche* that his readers then could translate on the basis of context (St&Su, 22–23; RS, 247; TrB, 57–60, 135).

Such patronizing assumptions of Brahmin superiority are not unique in Alger's juvenile work, for his books often apologize for the political and economic policies favored by the mugwump wing of the Republican Party. These sections of Alger's books may be considered reform tracts because they support proposals of the nostalgic, liberal reformers of the Gilded Age. Like them, for example, Alger feared that greenbacks, or fiat money backed only by government promises, and "free silver" were Democrat-inspired measures "calculated to lower the national credit or tarnish the national reputation for good faith," and against such "financial heresies" Alger hewed to the orthodox line. He praised Garfield as a "pronounced advocate of 'Honest Money'" (Canal, 251) and Webster as a soldier "in the battle for sound money" who helped defeat "a scheme to create an irredeemable paper currency" (Farm, 175). But in his biography of Lincoln, during whose administration greenbacks were first issued to help finance the Civil War, Alger remained silent on the subject of such money. Like other liberal Republicans, Alger defended neither a high protectionist tariff nor pure free trade, but a moderate tariff that would not disturb "the business interests of the country" (BacB, 117). He feared the consequences of imperialist annexation in the name of Manifest Destiny, believing that proponents of such schemes were impetuous Jacksonians whose carelessness might transform the nation from a peaceful defender of liberty into an aggressive power. The Mexican War, for example, he described as "ill-advised" (BacB, 117). And, again like other liberal Republicans, Alger was especially alarmed by the growth of political corruption. The villains in *Andy Gordon* (1881), *Struggling Upward* (1886), and *Luke Walton* (1887–88), and the snobs in *Digging for Gold* (1891) and *Rupert's Ambition* (1893–94) all harbor political ambitions, hoping to succeed in what Alger considered an arena corrupted by excessive self-interest and machine politics. He described Micky Maguire, an Irish bully in *Ragged Dick* (1867), as one who would have been "prominent at ward meetings, and a terror to respectable voters on election day" if he "interested himself in politics" (RD, 123). To correct the abuses that offended him, Alger proposed the simple remedy of moral reform.

On one other significant subject, the issue of capital punishment, Alger also shared the political prejudices of the liberal Republicans. Until the mid-1880s, Alger generally seemed to oppose capital punishment. He praised Lincoln, in the biography written in 1883, for the "infinite tenderness in the heart of this man which made him hard to consent to extreme punishment," and he mentioned specific instances when Lincoln's kind mercy saved young deserters from execution (BacB, 237), However, a change in Alger's attitude may be detected around the time of the Haymarket Square riot of 1886. The subsequent execution of four anarchists for allegedly inciting that riot may have inflamed the issue for Alger, much as it did for other liberal Republicans like E. L. Godkin. At any rate, by 1891, in *Digging for Gold*, Alger seemed to sanction the execution of a thief: "It seems hard to rejoice in the death of a fellow being," a virtuous character in that novel observes, "but no one can grieve over the taking off of such a man" (DG, 165). He identified the factor influencing his apparent change of heart in *A Cousin's Conspiracy* (1896): "Woe be to the offender who ventured to interfere with the rights of property" (CC, 140). Characteristically, Alger discussed the issue in a forum among characters in one of his books, *Lester's Luck* (1893). In this conversation, in which Alger's attitude may be identified with that of the ex-schoolmaster, he revealed his own ambivalent justification of capital punishment:

> "I don't believe in capital punishment," remarked the ex-schoolmaster.
> "You wouldn't have let him go free to rob and kill others?"
> "I would have put him in prison for life."
> "He was in prison, but broke out while he was awaiting trial—so, at least, I have heard. The man had no redeeming traits. He was an enemy of his kind, and deserved to die. So far as I had any part in his execution I feel no compunction. . . . He might have shot me, . . . like that young man we heard about. . . . And he might have ridden away with all our valuables. Our friend Mr. Brackett would hardly have liked that."
> "No, I can't say I should," said the ex-schoolmaster. "Theoretically I am opposed to capital punishment, but in the present instance, considering the desperate character and dark deeds of this man Brand, I am not sure but it was expedient to hang him." (LL, 295–96)

In short, Alger inflated the thin plot of many juvenile novels with a carefully measured political dimension that reinforced traditionally reverenced moral reforms popular among both antebellum Unitarians and postbellum liberal Republicans.

This discussion of Alger's fictional theory and literary models, his style and themes, his theory of human nature, and the social and political content of his juvenile fiction indicates that he wished to be considered primarily a teacher and moralist. The didactic tenor of his juvenile fiction harmonized several melodies—the Brahmin superiority of a Massachusetts patrician, the moral philosophy of a Harvard Unitarian, and the reform politics of a liberal Republican. Alger's belief that names and reputations should be deserved is ironic in light of the distortion his own reputation has suffered, for, hardly the teacher and moralist he wished to be considered, he has been regarded in recent decades primarily as a chorister who lauded economic triumph. Rather than singing a hymn of celebration set to this music, however, he used the same rigorous moral standards to appraise business activities that he had used to gauge success in country schoolrooms and city streets.

CHAPTER 5

Alger's Views toward Business

IN the decades following his death, after his books were no longer published and popularly read, Alger acquired a reputation as an apologist for business success and a purblind defender of the faith of orthodox capitalism. To be sure, Alger did offer in his juvenile fiction his opinions regarding the proper conduct of business, but, in general, these opinions were simply his application to business of the same moral principles that animate the whole of his fictional world. These principles of political economy were the standard Unitarian views toward business and commerce, and, unfortunately, their significance in Alger's juvenile fiction has been grossly distorted. Alger himself believed only that he was translating the technical language of political economy into entertaining stories for his juvenile audience; as he wrote in *Herbert Carter's Legacy* (1875), "Though political economy is generally studied in the junior or senior year at college, its principles, if familiarly illustrated, are not beyond the comprehension of a boy of fifteen" (HCL, 138). In other words, Alger the moral teacher attempted only to describe the universal principles of political economy in less esoteric language for his less sophisticated audience, not to create a mythology of business success.

I *Alger's Code of Good Business*

Alger's most succinct statement of his views toward business appears in a brief biographical sketch of the department-store magnate A. T. Stewart which he wrote in 1883 for the juvenile magazine *Golden Argosy* and which, unfortunately, has not been reprinted from that source. In this sketch Alger recorded "certain principles of business which Stewart adopted" as a young man, and from which he never deviated, to which we may attribute his subsequent fortune. These were: 1) Strict honesty in all dealings with customers. 2) One price for all. 3) Cash on delivery. 4) Business to be done as business, and without reference to any other consideration. 5) Courtesy to all, of whatever rank. In the days of his greatest prosperity a poor Irish woman was as welcome in his large store as a lady dressed in silks, and the clerk who should presume to treat her with impertinence would have been instantly discharged. All these rules I can unreservedly commend, with the exception of the fourth, which Mr. Stewart carried too far.

For example, as Alger explained, Stewart "was not a popular employer" because of the primacy of business considerations in his relations with others, and he "seldom tempered justice with mercy." Although Stewart is mentioned in more of his juvenile novels than any other historical figure, Alger declined to approve all of his business activities: "In many respects I cannot hold him up to the imitation of my readers. He was hard, stern, and neglected to do that good with his money which many far less wealthy have done. But he conducted his business, in the main, on the right principles, and deserved the success which he achieved."[1] In short, in this sketch Alger set down the code of good business he often subtly illustrated elsewhere in his work.

As a first commandment in that code, Alger contended that a merchant should deserve success by exercising such virtues as honesty. This simple contention masks his deep suspicion that, as he wrote in *Victor Vane* (1893), "In business as at present conducted a good many crooked things are done" (VV, 228). As one of his characters restated this notion, "When it comes to tradin', most everybody lies" (YMus, 21). Every allusion to "business" in Alger's *A Cousin's Conspiracy* (1896) refers to the bank thefts committed by a pair of dime-novelized James brothers in that book. Similarly, Alger associated "business" with counterfeiting in *Jack's Ward* (1875), kidnapping in *Frank and Fearless* (1885), and extortion in *Bob Burton* (1886–87). Alger's hero, on the other hand, has been bred and "trained to scrupulous honesty in money matters" (WBH, 247). In *Paul the Peddler* (1871), for example, the hero prefers to earn less in his business rather than turn to dishonest schemes to increase his sales. In his biography of Lincoln Alger noted that his subject's reputation for honesty had been acquired as a young storekeeper in Illinois and concluded that "mercantile honesty is some guarantee of political honesty" (BacB, 66).

Often implicit in Alger's praise of honesty in all business dealings is his belief that an employer, the purchaser of labor, is entitled to an honest day's work for an honest day's pay. In *The Store Boy* (1883–84) Alger explicitly linked business honesty and employee fidelity. As the hero of that novel concludes, "I think honesty and fidelity are good policy" (StB, 98). Although Alger often expressed sympathy for the working class, and especially for its underpaid members, he naively thought that an employee could improve his lot only by subscribing wholly to the interests of his employer. Consequently, recommendations of fidelity resound throughout his juvenile fiction. He described the patron in *Fame and Fortune* (1868), for example, as "an excellent business man, and very conscientious in the discharge of his duties. He required the same fidelity of others" (Fa&F, 62). Indeed, employers receive absolute loyalty from the heroes in these novels. The hero in *Frank and Fearless* (1885) prefers to die before he would violate the trust of his employer, and the hero of *A Debt of Honor* (1891), though hired by "a mean man," nevertheless resolves to "do what I can for him" (DofH, 221). Alger's blind endorsement of employee fidelity was a corollary of his basic assumption that merit would be rewarded by promotion. Alger's own generation, those Americans born around 1835 who matured during the period of rapid industrialization following the Civil War, probably enjoyed the highest rate of social mobility in this nation's history.[2] Alger acknowledged this rapid mobility in his fiction, although he exaggerated it in claiming, as he often did, that "The eminent men of the day, in all branches of business, and in all professions, were once poor boys" (StB, 52; cf. Grit, 198; YMus, 9). However, with his faith in merited promotion unchallenged, Alger could recommend without reservation that his readers become loyal employees. As he wrote in *Mark the Match Boy* (1869), "Those who fill subordinate positions acceptably are most likely to rise to stations where they will themselves have control over others" (MMB, 318). In other words, Alger tempted his readers to rise to respectability by offering them the carrot of eventual "control over others" if they served their employers faithfully. Believing that "an active, healthy boy seldom thinks of luxury, or craves it" (ATB, 158), he did not urge his readers to seek wealth. Indeed, as John G. Cawelti concludes, "Emphasis on fidelity to the employer's interests is perhaps the worst advice Alger could have given his young readers if financial success was of major interest to them."[3]

In his juvenile novels Alger also developed his reasons for endorsing Stewart's second principle of good business, the resolution to charge "one price for all." He subtly, though frequently, condemned excessive profiteering. In *Mark the Match Boy* (1869), for example, he criticized one character who "was not an advocate of the one-price system. He blacked boots for five cents when he could get no more. When he thought there was a reasonable prospect of getting ten cents, that was his price. Sometimes, as in the case of the young man from the rural districts, he advanced his fee to twenty-five cents. I don't approve Ben's system for my part. I think it savors considerably of sharp practice, and that fair prices in the long run are the best for all parties" (MMB, 289–90).

The phrase "fair prices" was not casually chosen by Alger, who in fact employed it or a similar phrase in over three dozen juvenile novels. A "fair price," as these contexts reveal, is not necessarily "market value;" whereas the former is determined by self-interest rightly considered, the latter is determined by self-interest untempered by the claims of conscience. In *Chester Rand* (1892), for example, the hero refuses to charge the highest possible price for some land he sells, and Alger approved his receipt of "a fair price" while retaining "the good will of the purchaser" (CR, 127). In *The Young Miner* (1879), on the other hand, a usurious squire seeks to purchase a farm at auction for its "market price," far less than "its intrinsic value" (YMin, 233), in effect cheating the hero and his family. Moreover, Alger consistently depicted pawnbrokers as selfish old men who "demand an extortionate profit" (PP, 86). In *Frank Hunter's Peril* (1885–86) he described the selfish pawnbroker as "a capitalist, who had for thirty-years lent money at usurious interest, taking advantage of a tight money market and the needs of embarrassed men" (FHP, 31). In such passages as this from *Luke Walton* (1887–88) Alger implied his consent to usury laws that would better protect the innocent poor from the evil designs of profiteers: "Though the New York pawnbroker is allowed to charge but three per cent a month, his Chicago associate charges more than three times as much" (LW, 246). Surprisingly, perhaps, he occasionally seemed to criticize the very idea of a profit motive and the machinations inherent in the marketplace. In *Tom Tracy* (1887) he described a retail clothing firm whose avaricious owners "usually aimed to get their clothing made for the lowest market prices, and to make the best possible bargain with the customers. The price of goods was fluctuating, and the easy going purchaser, unskilled in 'beating down,' usually paid an excessive price for his goods" (TTr, 42).

Just as Alger called for "fair prices," so too did he defend the notion of a "just wage." As Michael Zuckerman has correctly observed, in Alger's books the prices the characters pay and the wages they receive are "often determined by consideration and decency" rather than supply and demand.[4] In over three dozen juvenile novels Alger criticized payment of "low" or "starvation wages" to workers and/or proposed that they receive "just" or "respectable wages." In *Phil the Fiddler* (1872), for example, he noted "the essential injustice of laboring without proper compensation" (PF, 317). Although he once suggested that "a dollar a day" represented "fair pay" for a teen-aged boy (ETB, 27), he best expressed his moral outrage at the exploitation of labor in numerous references to the "starvation wages paid to toiling women" (ANY, 35), particularly to seamstresses. The mother of the hero in *Luke Walton* (1887–88) estimates her income for sewing shirts at only "three cents an hour" (LW, 18), and the highest wage paid to any seamstress in these books barely covers the expense of her rent and food.

In Alger's fictional world the fundamental, structural obstacle to establishing prices and wages according to standards of equity and decency seems to be, significantly enough, economic competition. Alger's second reason, then, for endorsing Stewart's "one price for all" rule, likewise developed in his juvenile books, was his belief that economic competition is both inefficient and dehumanizing. In Alger's view, when too many sellers of the same product—whether material or labor—compete in the marketplace, they all suffer a common fate: low prices and economic hardship. Alger best developed his critique of business competition in *Paul the Peddler* (1871), the first chapter of which offers a sound lesson in laissez-faire economics:

Street boys are as enterprising, and have as sharp eyes for business as their elders, and no one among them can monopolize a profitable business long. This is especially the case with the young street merchant. When one has had the good luck to find some attractive article which promises to sell briskly, he takes every care to hide the source of his supply from his rivals in trade. But this is almost impossible. Cases are frequent where such boys are subjected to the closest espionage, their steps being dogged for hours by boys who think they have found a good thing and are determined to share it. In the present case Paul had hit upon an idea which seemed to promise well, and he was determined to keep it to himself as long as possible. As soon as he was subjected to competition and rivalry his gains would probably diminish. (PP, 5–6)

When a cutthroat competitor enters the same prize-package business as the hero, he spoils it for both of them: "His new competitor monopolized the trade, and for two hours Paul did not get a solitary customer" (PP, 15). Paul is forced to move to another, less desirable location, where his profits are substantially reduced: "He had made more than double as much the day before in less time; but then he did not suffer from competition. He began to doubt whether he could long pursue this business, since other competitors were likely to spring up" (PP, 17). Similarly, Paul's mother, because of a surplus of seamstresses, sews shirts for about twenty-five cents per day, although the same shirts are sold at retail for "five times the price Mrs. Hoffman had been accustomed to receive" for making them (PP, 52). Fortunately, before the end of the novel both Paul and his mother conclude more favorable business arrangements. Alger's critique of competition in business, however, would reappear in other, later works. In *Five Hundred Dollars* (1888–89), for example, the enterprising hero suffers from competition: "Bert continued to pick berries, but the price fell rapidly until it touched six cents, and it was not so easy to sell berries at all, for many others engaged in picking them, and the market was overstocked" ($500, 73). On the other hand, the newsboy hero of *Luke Walton* (1887–88) experiences the "advantage of diminished competition" (LW, 35) when two other newsboys leave the market.

Similarly, Alger recognized that unorganized workers would compete among themselves for available jobs, thus depressing the wages of all. Because "there are too many poor women who are ready to work for starvation wages," he explained, all seamstresses had suffered (ANY, 122). In *The World Before Him* (1880) he noted that "those who know how many dry goods clerks there always are seeking employment" would understand how an employer could obtain clerks for low wages (WBH, 209). And the hero in *Adrift in the City* (1887), vainly seeking a position that would pay him at least six dollars a week, finally is offered a job for only two dollars a week because "times were hard" and "there were thousands out of employment, and fifty applications where there was one vacancy" (AC, 148).

Because of the adverse effects of competition among individual workers, Alger subtly advocated organization of the working class, hardly a popular opinion among Protestant ministers during the Gilded Age. Without an organization to represent their interests, however, "poor sewing girls" who were "employed for a pittance," according to Alger, "were not so well able to defend themselves against imposition" (BLB, 245). He at least once expressed sympathy in a juvenile novel for "the toiling thousands who are interested in the passage of eight-hour laws" (Sl&S, 138). He contended in *Dan the Newsboy* (1880) that "money always has [the decided advantage] when pitted against labor" (DN, 31), and in *Slow and Sure* (1872) he offered "an illustration, on a small scale, of the advantage of capital. The lucky possessor of two or three extra blacking-boxes has it in his power to derive quite a revenue [by charging the boys who sub-contract their use]. As a general thing such contracts, however burdensome to one party, are faithfully kept. It might be supposed that boys of ordinary shrewdness would as soon as possible save up enough to buy a box and brush of their own; but as they only receive half-profits, that is not easy, after defraying expenses of lodging and meals" (Sl&S, 98). In other words, Alger agreed that a wage earner faced a nearly insurmountable task if he wished to begin his own business. As he concluded in *The Erie Train Boy* (1890), "A man must have money to take money" (ETB, 8). Rather than compete for positions and promotions, Alger's heroes wish aloud that their brother workmen could "get as high pay as I do" (TomB, 124). And on six different occasions, first in *Wait and Hope* (1877), published during the most turbulent year in American labor history, Alger quoted the biblical adage "the worker is worthy of his hire" to defend the right of all workers to a just wage.

In his juvenile fiction Alger also developed Stewart's third principle of good business, the decidedly moral advice that one should pay for goods received with cash and thus avoid debt. Frequently, as in *Bound to Rise* (1873) and *Mark Mason's Victory* (1892), the snob incurs a large debt with a tailor so that he can dress fashionably. In all such cases, of course, his irresponsible conduct contrasts with the hero's firm resolve to "pay cash" (BR, 70). Indeed, the hero believes it is "a crazy idea to run into debt for an expensive suit" (MMV, 202). In short, as Alger wrote in *Struggling Upward* (1886), "I am disposed to think that a boy's worst enemy is the one who makes it easy for him to run into debt. . . . The day of reckoning always comes in such cases, as I hope my young friends will fully understand. Debt is much more easily contracted than liquidated" (SU, 85, 86). When a hero is compelled by circumstance to borrow, as in *Joe's Luck* (1878), he erases his debt as quickly as possible. Moreover, like the authors of more traditional success manuals, Alger cautioned his readers against co-signing notes for friends or relatives. Three juvenile novels written late in his career contain otherwise admirable characters who, after foolishly endorsing others' notes, suffer bankruptcy (CUB, 191; AGP, 9; CC, 22).

Alger believed Stewart had obeyed too slavishly his fourth rule, that business should be conducted without regard to other considerations. Only evil squires justify their selfishness in his juvenile books with the claim that "business is business"—indeed, Alger noted in *Andy Grant's Pluck* (1895) that "these words are used as an excuse for a great many mean acts" (AGP, 241). Alger developed his dissent fom Stewart's "business is business" rule, first, by idealizing the moral certainties of a pre-industrial economy. As Richard Weiss has noted, "Correctly understood, Alger is not a representative of his time, but a nostalgic spokesman of a dying order. Of middle-class rural origins, he was always an alien in the industrially dominated society of his adulthood. . . . Alger's work reflects an attempt to re-create the more harmonious society in which he was raised. His heroes come from another time, another society, another reality. Rather than extolling the dominant values of his day, he was reacting against them."[5] Or as Cawelti suggests, Alger's fictional world represented "a throwback to the economic life of an earlier period, when American business was still dominated by merchants whose economic behavior in retrospect seemed refined and benevolent in comparison to the devastating strategies of transcontinental railroad builders, iron and steel manufacturers, and other corporate giants."[6] Most of Alger's juvenile novels are set before the Civil War,[7] many of them in small New England or Midwestern villages, and virtually all of the manual occupations mentioned in them— carpenter, fisherman, furniture maker, and so forth—are nonindustrial. When Alger did mention a factory or a mill in his fiction, he invariably referred to a plant employing a pre-industrial, unmechanical means of production—brick factories in *Brave and Bold* (1872) and *Wait and Hope* (1877), a furniture factory in *Driven from Home* (1889), a water-powered mill for the manufacture of leather board in *Ben Bruce* (1892–93), and, most often, unmechanized shoe factories modeled after those in use in Marlborough, Massachusetts, when Alger lived there as a boy. His descriptions of these factories merit special attention, for they indicate both a thorough knowledge of the shoe business before the Civil War and his idealization of that seemingly simpler, more benign era.

In about a dozen juvenile novels Alger's hero works as a pegger in a shoe factory located in a New England village. The hero of *Tom Thatcher's Fortune* (1882), for example, "was employed ten hours a day in pegging shoes, for the lucrative sum of fifty cents per day" (TTF, 5). Because the manufacture of shoes before the introduction in the 1860s of such devices as the McKay pegging machine required a large manual labor force, the shoe business was susceptible to cyclical fluctuations. As Alger explained in *Bound to Rise* (1873), "the worst of the shoe trade" is that "it isn't steady. When it's good everybody rushes into it, and the market soon gets overstocked. Then there's no work for weeks" (BR, 100). In other words, employment in pre-industrial shoe manufacture, upon which depended the economies of many New England towns, was not very reliable. During the economic panic of 1837, dozens of Massachusetts shoe factories employing thousands of workers simply closed their doors.[8] In short, when the heroes of *Luck and Pluck* (1869) and *Mark Manning's Mission* (1894) lose their pegging jobs because of prior overproduction, Alger was describing their plight realistically.

The solution to cyclical unemployment in the shoe business was industrialization, specifically the widespread adoption of the steam-powered pegging machine, which made possible "uniformity of output, economy of time, labor, and stock."[9] Unfortunately, however, mechanization also reduced the number of jobs in shoe manufacturing. Alger failed to appreciate how this development was a stabilizing influence on the shoe industry after the Civil War. Rather, he oversimplified the alternatives and, with an unambiguous choice between the idealized past and inhumane present, implied that mechanization was a villainous strategy devised to increase profits by reducing employment. He best illustrated this opinion in *Five Hundred Dollars* (1888–89), in which the hero loses his job in the local shoe factory to a pegging machine. The selfish owner justifies his action as a "business necessity," claiming that the machine "will do the work cheaper and more effectually than under the present system." The hero's kind mother, a nascent New England Luddite, who admits that she does not "know about business," laments, "Oh, why couldn't you have let matters remain as they were? You may gain something, but you are depriving the boys of their livelihood" ($500, 57–58). Nostalgically idealizing the easy moral choices of a pre-industrial age, Alger refused to accept "business necessity" as an excuse for the inhumanity of businessmen.

Alger developed his dissent from the normal business ethic, secondly, by introducing into his juvenile fiction the distinction between the organic community, in which each member is a part of an interrelated whole, and the impersonal market economy, in which relationships are merely economic transactions and each person is valued only as a producer and consumer. As Howe explains, the distinction was familiar to the Harvard Unitarians, for whom "the ideal commonwealth was an organic unit, composed, like a living body, of interrelated parts, each contributing its essential function."[10] Alger offered three models of the organic community in his juvenile fiction: the family, the farming community, and the company of cooperative street urchins, usually the residents of the Newsboys' Lodging House. In turn, he contrasted each of them with a less desirable market economy. In *The Cash Boy* (1875), for example, he contrasted the "sacred bond of affection" uniting the hero and his mother (CB, 42) with the "mercenary . . . tie that bound [the snob] to his aunt" (CB, 105). In *Bound to Rise* (1873) he contrasted the love shared by the hero and his father with the exploitation of the snob by his father, who "wanted to convert him into a money-making machine—a mere drudge, working him hard, and denying him, as long as he could, even the common recreations of boyhood" (BR, 15). Similarly, Alger contrasted the neighborly cooperation of the ideal farming community with one tainted by commercialism in a dialogue between a mercenary squire and a farmer in *The Young Miner* (1879):

"Suppose I should foreclose—you would consider it an unkind thing and a great hardship, wouldn't you?"
"It would take away my means of supporting my family. I don't think you would go to extremes, for the sake of thirty dollars."
"It isn't the amount of money, neighbor Nelson, that is to be considered. It is the principle that is involved."
This is a very common pretext with men who have made up their minds to do a mean thing. Generally speaking, it is false, and the money is the first consideration. . . .
"I don't see how any principle is involved, Squire Hudson."

"You look at the matter solely from a debtor's point of view. If you held the mortgage, instead of myself, you would change your view very quickly."

"I don't think I should," said the farmer slowly. "I would be considerate to a poor neighbor, even if it did inconvenience me a little. (YMin, 161–62, 164)

Finally, Alger contrasted the cooperative spirit of most street boys, who profess no interest in using others "to make money" (MMB, 220), with the business relationships among other, less virtuous characters. In novels such as *Five Hundred Dollars* (1888–89) he idealized the organic community among boys in the less stratified society of his own youth, when "all the boys were friendly and sociable, no matter whether they were rich or poor" ($500, 18). On the other hand, in novels such as *Cast Upon the Breakers* (1893) two selfish boys experience a sudden rift because their "intimacy . . . had grown out of business considerations" (CUB, 143).

Alger best illustrated the difference between the organic community and the market economy in his juvenile novel *Dan the Newsboy* (1880), which is thematically devoted to contrasting the intimacy of family and friends with other relationships governed solely by business considerations. In this novel the hero and his mother endure the injustices perpetrated by the mother's employer, Mr. Gripp, and their landlord, Mr. Grabb, whose relationships with others are simple economic transactions. Gripp, the owner of a clothing store, pays his seamstresses only about twenty cents per day in order that he "might wax rich, and live in good style up town" (DN, 25). The hero, intuitively realizing that "there's a difference in earning and being paid," complains that Gripp "is making a fortune out of those who sew for him" (DN, 21). Similarly, Grabb mercilessly evicts tenants in mid-winter if he cannot exact their rent, and justifies his callousness as "business" (DN, 50, 53). However, on two separate occasions charitable strangers motivated only by a sense of obligation to others rescue the hero and his mother from financial exigency. At the end of the novel, one even adopts the hero and sends him to college, and installs his mother in her home as "housekeeper and friend," because she is "quite sure we can all live happily together" (DN, 287). In light of Alger's idealization of the organic community, this interest in the principle of economic cooperation is hardly surprising.

As an advocate of shared responsibility among members of a

community, Alger at least tentatively addressed two questions relevant to his readers: Who is responsible for exploiting those workers who are paid starvation wages, and who or what is responsible for the loss of employment during periods of economic recession? In response to the first question Alger formulated a doctrine of complicity like that advanced by W. D. Howells in his social novels, especially *The Minister's Charge* and *A Hazard of New Fortunes*. Briefly summarized, Alger with this doctrine indicated that consumers of cheap goods produced by underpaid workers share responsibility with the employers who profit by selling those goods. The rationalization offered by one employer, that he pays low wages because he operates on a thin profit margin, meets with a direct rebuke: "Then charge enough to afford respectable wages" (TTr, 51). In *A Rolling Stone* (1894), similarly, a gentleman refuses to purchase a suit when he learns that the clothing store underpays its employees. "I have a rule," he explains, "never to trade at a store where such meannesses are practiced" (RS, 257).

Unfortunately, Alger, seemingly perplexed by the second question, failed to affix responsibility for loss of employment during recessions. He did recognize the severity of the problem, however, referring in about two dozen novels to periods of "dull business" and high unemployment. And he at least mentioned in his fiction every major economic catastrophe which occurred during his life, including the Panics of 1837, 1857, 1867, 1873, and 1893 (cf. YO, 105; CB, 26; SH, 51; CUB, 40; YS, 132). In other words, it is inaccurate to allege, as critics occasionally do, that "the Algerian world of business was undisturbed by depressions."[11] For example, Alger set *Jack's Ward* (1875) "in the year 1867, memorable for its panic, and the business depression which followed. Nearly every branch of industry suffered and thousands of men were thrown out of work, and utterly unable to find employment of any kind" (JW, 4). Similarly, in *Rupert's Ambition* (1893–94), written during the Panic of 1893, Alger acknowledged that during a "general depression of business" (RA, 83) the individual is subjected to the whims of chance in his struggle to rise. In the first chapter of this novel the hero loses his sales job because of "the dullness in business" (RA, 2), but he does not know what has caused his loss: "It is only because business is dull that I have to go. I can't blame the firm" (RA, 11). In short, Alger failed to isolate a structural source of economic depression, although he admitted that economic conditions beyond the control of the individual affected opportunities to enter the occupational mainstream. In one of his next novels, then, the hero makes "application for a hundred situations" although "his luck does not improve" because of the "general business depression which made employers adverse to hiring new employees" (YS, 132). The supposed advocate of free enterprise apparently had begun to fear that the Invisible Hand had become paralyzed.

Alger recurrently illustrated in his juvenile fiction Stewart's fifth and final rule of good business, that all customers, whatever their social rank, are entitled to courtesy and respect. The benevolent patron in *Helping Himself* (1884–85) "was just as polite to a boy as to his best customer. This is, I am quite aware," Alger concluded, "an unusual trait, and, therefore, the more to be appreciated when we meet with it" (HH, 54). Common courtesy, rather than social rank or sales potential, also governs the hero's treatment of customers in *Strong and Steady* (1871) and *Chester Rand* (1892).

In addition to endorsing a five-point code of good business, Alger indicated in his biographical sketch of Stewart that a prosperous businessman ought to be a good steward of his wealth. As Howe has observed, this notion was common among the Unitarian moralists, who "never let the Boston merchants forget that responsibilities as well as privileges went with wealth and status."[12] Alger likewise illustrated the assumption of these responsibilities in his juvenile books. As he wrote in one, "A rich man owes a debt to the world, and should try to liquidate it by doing all the good in his power" (TrB, 187). For example, the patron in *Brave and Bold* (1872) announces that because "God has blessed me with abundant means . . . it is only right that I should employ a portion in His service" (B&B, 216). Alger contended that the prosperous businessman ought to use his wealth to do good; that is, that his self-interest should promote the common interest. "The wealth of Amos Lawrence and Peter Cooper was a source of blessing to mankind," he noted in one juvenile novel (StB, 68). Significantly, however, those businessmen Alger approvingly mentioned most often in his books—Stewart, Lawrence, Cooper, John Jacob Astor, and Commodore Vanderbilt—all had accumulated their wealth while Alger was still a young man. Though a modern reader familiar only with his reputation might suppose that he at least alluded to the more recent success stories of such millionaire-industrialists as Andrew Carnegie and John D. Rockefeller, and perhaps even modeled heroes after them, Alger in fact conspicuously ignored them. He apparently idealized the faithful stewardship of the old-fashioned merchants and financiers, not the well-publicized "philanthropy" of the robber barons.

Nearly identical episodes in three juvenile novels written at intervals of about a decade serve to elaborate Alger's doctrine of stewardship and his implicit condemnation of the parsimonious plutocrats of his own day. In the earliest of these novels, *Brave and Bold* (1872), the hero spies a boulder on a railroad track shortly before a passenger train is scheduled to pass. He rushes in the direction of the approaching train, flags its engineer to stop, and thus saves all the passengers onboard from certain death. They gratefully reward him with enough money to rescue his family from imminent eviction (B&B, 133). A similar episode occurs in *Facing the World* (1885). In this case, the "president and leading stockholder of the road," one of those saved, contributes twenty dollars of the hero's reward and collects the others' contributions in his own hat. "Make good use" of the money, he advises the hero. "I shall owe you a considerable balance, for I value my life at more than twenty dollars. . . . If you ever need a friend, or a service, call on me" (FW, 22). A faithful steward, this patron gains the respect of the hero, who subsequently entrusts his reward to his safekeeping. In the third version of this incident, in *Digging for Gold* (1891), the hero again warns the engineer of danger to his train, thus saving the lives of the passengers and earning a reward. But a significant difference occurs in this final rendition of the scene:

The passengers generally brought forward their contributions, though some were able to give but a silver coin. There was one notable exception: One man, when he saw what was going forward, quietly shrank away, and got back into the train.

"Who's that man?" asked the engineer sharply.

"I know," said an Irishman, who out of his poverty had given a dollar. "It's Mr. Leonard Buckley, of New York. He's worth a million. He is rich enough to buy us all up."

"No matter how much money he possesses, he is a poor man," said the minister significantly.

"He's given all his life is worth to the world," said a passenger cynically. "When he dies he won't be missed." (DG, 18)

This condemnation of parsimony among wealthy businessmen is characteristic of Alger's juvenile novels, especially those written late in his career, and is rooted in his idea of stewardship. Although he would not have claimed that money is unimportant, his code of good business and idea of stewardship evince his opinion that the highest values are moral, not monetary.

II *"Money is the Root of All Evil"*

In his juvenile fiction Alger offered a broad critique of money as a measure of value and status. In the themes of the Rise to Respectability and Beauty versus Money, discussed in an earlier chapter, Alger attributed relatively minor or secondary importance to money, compared to the greater claims of Respectability and Beauty. But these two themes, though they suggest the depth of Alger's critique of money and the business considerations it engenders, fail to indicate its breadth. Not only did Alger criticize the quest for business success from a variety of perspectives, he carefully qualified his description of his hero's quest in order to avoid sanctioning the accumulation of money through business dealings. Characteristically, Alger illustrated the contrasting opinions regarding the value of money in a debate between two characters, an intemperate woman and the hero:

"It's a good thing to have money," said the woman, more to herself than to Walter.

"Yes," said Walter, "it's very convenient to have money; but there are other things that are better."

"Such as what?" demanded the woman abruptly.

"Good health for one thing."

"What else?"

"A good conscience."

She laughed scornfully. "I'll tell you there's nothing so good as money. I've wanted it all my life, and never could get it. . . . Money is sure to do good, no matter how it comes," said the woman, fiercely. "Think of what it will buy! A comfortable home, ease, luxury, respect. Some time before I die I hope to have as much as I want."

"I hope you will," said Walter; "but I don't think you will find it as powerful as you think." (St&St, 268, 318)

Anticipating the tendency among more modern success theorists who emphasize health rather than wealth, Alger consistently argued in his juvenile books that "Health is a blessing not to be overestimated. It is better than money" (D&D, 29). Moreover, he noted that the accumulation of money through business often destroys health; the constitution of a character in *Frank and Fearless* (1885), for example, "had been undermined years before by a residence in Central America, where he had acquired a fortune, but paid a costly price therefor in the loss of his health" (Fr&F, 41). Emphasizing the importance of health over wealth, Alger did not conceal his disdain for those businessmen who reverse their priority.

Although Alger was not as acerbic a social critic as Thorstein Veblen, passages from Alger's juvenile fiction can be used to illustrate many of the same indictments of the barbaric business culture leveled by Veblen in *The Theory of the Leisure Class* (1899). Surprisingly, perhaps, Alger shared with Veblen a fear that the rich would "get richer and the poor get poorer." In *The Young Adventurer* (1878), for example, the hero's virtuous father, who labors under the lion's paw, complains "that money should be so unevenly distributed" (YAd, 5). Similarly, the father of the hero in *A Debt of Honor* (1891) laments "how unequally fortune is distributed!" (DofH, 33). Alger elsewhere hedged on this point, as in *Driven from Home* (1889), in which he voiced a suspicion that although "there are doubtless inequalities of fortune," they are "not as great as many like to represent" (DfH, 193). Still, Alger, like Veblen, seemed genuinely concerned by the inexplicable and growing disparity between rich and poor.

Moreover, Alger illustrated four other Veblenian doctrines in addition to the two—the "pecuniary canons of taste" of the snobs and the "instinct of workmanship" of the heroes—discussed in an earlier chapter. For example, he illustrated "pecuniary emulation" among the barbaric success-worshippers in *Tom the Bootblack* (1873): "Such is the influence of wealth" upon the disposition of the snob that he "made up his mind that he had better change his manner" toward a rich acquaintance (TomB, 116). Alger also illustrated the "conspicuous leisure" of the barbaric upper class. The wealthy villain in *The Young Explorer* (1880) "had plenty to live upon and nothing in particular to do, except to look after his property. He was a portly man, who walked with a slow, dignified step, leaning on a gold-headed cane, and evidently felt his importance" (YEx, 23). Thirdly, Alger recognized in dozens of his juvenile books what Veblen later labeled "conspicuous consumption." In only one example, from *A Debt of Honor* (1891), the villain "lived in quite the most pretentious house. . . . All that money could buy within reasonable limits was his. Handsome furniture, fine engravings, expensive paintings, a stately carriage and handsome horses, contributed to make life comfortable and desirable" (DofH, 116). Finally, Alger recurrently illustrated the corrupted "belief in luck" among the leisure class by criticizing Wall Street speculation as a species of gambling. Particularly after financial panics depressed the market, he characterized those who believe in lucky stock investments as foolish. In *Victor Vane* (1893), a character who "expected to double his money" by sending it "to a broker in Wall Street" instead lost every cent (VV, 344). Similarly, a banker in *Andy Grant's Pluck* (1895) admits that "In a moment of madness" he risked money in Wall Street. "I lost and went in deeper, hoping to be more fortunate. . . . That is the way such things usually happen" (AGP, 12). In short, Alger offered a dissenting opinion of the quest for business success, one which judged the leisure class by the standard of moral, not financial, accountability.

Alger profoundly distrusted any behavior that was motivated by the desire to accumulate money. As a Unitarian minister and writer of didactic fiction, he was fond of quoting the biblical verse "the love of money is the root of all evil," to which he alluded in more than a dozen juvenile novels. He condemned the sin of avarice and "that greed of gain which hardens the heart and banishes all scruples" (INW, 182) with evangelical fervor. His strongest condemnation of a character was his declaration, as in *Chester Rand* (1892), that "He has made money his god, and serves his chosen deity faithfully" (CR, 15). Alger often used three stock characters—the patron, the villain, and the hero—as vehicles for his condemnation of avarice and greed in business. The patron, usually wealthy and often a businessman, never covets greater wealth. "I am not anxious to become richer, having enough for all my needs," one of them declares (D&D, 103). Similarly, the patron in *Digging for Gold* (1891) explains that after he had "secured all I needed for my modest wants . . . I stopped, for I had no object in accumulating more" (DG, 121). On the other hand, the villain, who acts as the patron's foil in the structure of the novel, invariably is portrayed as avaricious. Ironically, the villains are the only self-made men Alger depicted in his fiction, for he equated "self-made" with "selfish." In *The Erie Train Boy* (1890), for example, the villain "had an income of four thousand dollars a year from rents. He was now sixty years of age. At twenty-one he was working for eight dollars a week, and saving three-fifths of that. By slow degrees he had made himself rich, but in so doing he had denied himself all but the barest necessaries. . . . It was his great enjoyment to see his hoards annually increasing, and he had no mercy for needy or unfortunate tenants who found themselves unable to pay their rent promptly" (ETB, 20). The self-made villains do not merit Alger's praise, but his censure, and these commercial characters are denied the sympathy of neighbors and relatives. Wealth is not necessarily a badge of virtue, especially in Alger's later novels, for he concluded that Fortune "does not always favor the brave, but often helps the undeserving" (DN, 218).

Alger carefully qualified the rise of the third character, his hero, so that he would not appear to be sanctioning moneymaking alone. First, as a member of an organic community, the hero cannot be accurately characterized as "self-made." Indeed, as Michael Zuckerman has noted, "Not one of Alger's elect is ever self-employed at the end of a novel, nor do any of them really wish to be."[13] Secondly, the hero, like his patron, is interested only in earning a competence or a "sufficiency of this world's goods" (YS, 50), not in accumulating a fortune. The country-boy hero of A Boy's Fortune (1889), when asked if he travels to the city to seek his fortune, replies, "If I can make a living it is all I expect" (BF, 5). Alger refused, especially in his pre-1890 novels, to hoist his hero to the top of the economic ladder, and instead continually insisted that wealth is a relative status. "Wealth is comparative," he wrote in Ragged Dick (1867), "and Dick probably felt as rich [with about a hundred dollars] as many men who are worth a hundred thousand dollars" (RD, 177). His moral heroes with their rather meager rewards feel rich, as in Slow and Sure (1872): With "five dollars in his pocket . . . Julius felt as rich as Stewart or Vanderbilt" (Sl&S, 202). The hero of Chester Rand (1892) claims that "I shall feel rich earning seven dollars per week" as a mailing clerk (CR, 117). As late as 1895, in Andy Grant's Pluck, Alger wrote that "the prospect of earning nine dollars a week" made the hero "feel like a millionaire" (AGP, 45). By asserting that wealth is relative, Alger was able to ignore for most of his career the incredible business success enjoyed by the Gilded Age industrialists. Thirdly, Alger qualified his hero's quest for success by emphasizing his selfless motive. He wishes to rise not to satisfy a gnawing hunger for self-aggrandizement, but in order to be better equipped to help others, particularly his parents. Finally, Alger warned his readers that the hero's good fortune is exceptional, not typical. As he wrote in *Victor Vane* (1893), "I do not wish my boy readers to look forward to the probability of equal good fortune. Let Victor's example stimulate them to equal fidelity and they are sure to attain a fair measure of success" (VV, 337). Not everyone will succeed, Alger averred, however happy his home and refined his habits.

In only one significant way was Alger influenced in the course of his long career by the popular image of the success enjoyed by the millionaire-industrialists like Carnegie and Rockefeller. As a result of his accommodation—not his contribution—to the success mythology of the Gilded Age, the rewards earned by his heroes are far greater in the novels he wrote after about 1889–90 than in the ones he wrote prior to that date. In his earliest novels the hero aspires to a respectable middle-class career as an accountant or salesman rather than to exorbitant wealth. Ragged Dick, for example, hopes merely to leave boot-blacking and engage in respectable enterprise, even if this means reducing his income. He frequently voices his mercantile dream, which is realized by the novel's end. The rewards won by the heroes of other early Alger juveniles are similarly benign. At the end of the misleadingly entitled *Fame and Fortune* (1868), the hero possesses an income of fourteen hundred dollars per year plus interest on about two thousand dollars. *Paul the Peddler* (1871) ends with the hero in possession of two hundred and fifty dollars, almost the exact sum necessary to stave off his family's eviction, and a necktie stand from which he hopes to milk ten to fifteen dollars each week. *Phil the Fiddler* (1872) closes as Phil, rescued nearly frozen from a snow drift and nursed to health by an elderly doctor and his wife, decides to remain with his foster parents. As late as 1886, in *Struggling Upward*, the hero acquires an aggregate fortune of only about ten thousand dollars. However, after about 1889–90, the hero acquires a stupendous fortune or, even more incredibly, a fiefdom. Alger continued to offer the four qualifications to the hero's quest—by noting his reliance on the help of others, his modest aspirations, his selfless motive, and the exceptional nature of his rise—but substantially increased the size of his reward. Much as he earlier had hoped to stem the decline in his popularity by adapting the violence and Western setting of the dime novel to his moral tale, Alger apparently hoped after 1889–90 to increase sales by accommodating the stranger-than-fiction success stories of the Gilded Age millionaires.

The hero of *Adrift in New York* (1889), for example, is reinstated at the end of that novel to his position as heir to four hundred thousand dollars. The same plot device obtains in *A Cousin's Conspiracy* (1896), in which the hero acquires a hundred thousand dollars and a claim to a quarter of a million. In *Digging for Gold* (1891) the hero invests a modest sum in land around which the city of San Francisco mushrooms. In only five years, Alger concluded, he "will be a rich man" (DG, 197). Perhaps the most extreme example of the later, exaggerated reward appears in *Jed the Poorhouse Boy* (1892). Incredibly transformed at the end of the novel into Sir Robert Fenwick of England, the hero possesses an ancestral estate and an annual income of twenty-five thousand dollars. Whereas in the early Alger juveniles the hero must capitalize on his opportunities by rescuing a drowning child or returning a lost billfold, in the later books the hero enjoys Good Fortune as though he has been chosen by an inexorable fate to succeed. Ironically, these later novels with their fantastic endings did stem Alger's sales decline— albeit a generation too late—because they were probably the most popularly reprinted of his books during the period of his greatest sales early in the twentieth century. In other words, Alger may have acquired his modern reputation at least partly because an unrepresentative selection of his juvenile books became popular.

III   *Alger's Condemnation of the Robber Barons*

A survey of Alger's juvenile novels by date of composition also reveals a number of subtle allusions to contemporary business practices. Always measuring these practices with the ruler of morality, Alger often issued in his fiction thinly disguised condemnations of specific business schemes. Unfortunately, these allusions have usually gone unnoticed, both because no reliable composition dates for the books had been established until recently and because modern readers, even when dates were available, did not consider the books as period documents which might mention actual events. In fact, Alger specifically alluded to four notoriously corrupt commercial schemes in his juvenile fiction. First, he recognized that, their rhetoric about competition notwithstanding, the major industrialists of his day formed combinations—pools, trusts, holding companies, corporations, or mergers—to circumvent price-cutting and reduced profits. For example, the evil capitalist who stalks the pages of *Walter Griffith* (1887), written only ten years after Rockefeller invented the trust and soon after the appearance of the salt, leather, and sugar trusts, "frowned at the suggestion of competition" (WG, 222). Rather than compete, Alger explained, "the bigger boys" could do as they wished if only they "formed a combination" (BBA, 38).

Secondly, Alger often obliquely criticized the policies of rebates, "midnight tariffs," and special rate concessions granted to companies, especially Standard Oil, by railroad lines. Soon after the Hepburn Committee investigation, mandated by the New York State legislature, first revealed in 1879 the widespread abuse of rebates, Alger joined the popular chorus of protests about this practice. In *The Train Boy* (1883), for example, a villainous accountant tries to obtain a well-paying job for his nephew because the nephew "had agreed to pay him a commission of two dollars a week, which the book-keeper, being fond of money, was not above accepting" (TrB, 212). Even as the Cullom Committee of the U.S. Senate, responding to popular outrage, investigated the problem of federal regulation of the railroads and recommended legislation banning rebates, Alger described the scheme on a domestic scale in an 1886 novel: "Mrs. Mercer, the housekeeper, . . . bought everything for the house, and levied tribute from every tradesman as a compensation for turning the trade in his direction. The result was that [the consumer] Mrs. Granville, without being aware of it, paid a larger price than any one else for what articles she purchased, the storekeeper and others compensating themselves in this way for the percentage they had to pay the housekeeper" (ATB, 173). Five years after the passage of the Interstate Commerce Act, Alger remained critical of the outlawed rebate. In *Jed* (1892) Squire Dixon, as a function of public trust, is empowered to appoint the Overseer of the Poor; although he is a rich man, he selfishly "accepts five dollars a month from the man he installed in office" (JPB, 408).

Thirdly, Alger condemned stock manipulations like those notoriously practiced by Jay Gould and his confederates. Occasionally, Alger explicitly criticized Gould's stock technique of profits through destruction, as in *The Store Boy* (1883–84), in which a character who has lost money in stock speculation accuses "Keene or Jay Gould or some of those big fellows" of upsetting the market (StB, 153). (Alger is probably referring here to Keene and Gould's manipulation of Union Pacific stock in 1879. As Matthew Josephson writes, basing his account on contemporary newspaper stories, Gould arranged for the circulation of "exuberant reports of the company's financial progress" and as a result "widows and orphans and lady stockholders rushed to buy the stock." After artificially inflating the price by increasing demand for the stock, Gould quietly unloaded most of his own shares and reaped a windfall profit of about ten million dollars.[14]) In *Luke Walton* (1887–88) Alger again alluded to this nefarious scheme. Robber baron Thomas Browning, a character probably modeled upon Gould, explains the stock swindle by which he profited: With a modest original investment, "I hired an office, printed circulars, distributed glowing accounts of imaginary wealth, etc. It cost me considerable for advertising, but I sold seventy thousand shares, and when I had gathered in the money I let the bottom fall out. There was a great fuss, of course, but I figured as the largest loser, being the owner of thirty thousand shares (for which I hadn't paid a cent), and so shared the sympathy extended to losers. It was a nice scheme, and after deducting all expenses, I made a clean seventy-five thousand dollars out of it" (LW, 115). Later, a widow who had invested and lost her entire estate of five thousand dollars, bequeathed by her dead husband to support her and two children, comes to Browning to plead her cause. "One of your circulars fell into my hands," she says. "You endorsed all that the circular contained. You said that within a year the shares which were two dollars each would rise to at least ten dollars. So I invested all the money I had. You know what followed. In six months the shares went down to nothing and I found myself penniless. . . . But you seem to be a rich man" (LW, 117). Despite her plea to be partly reimbursed for her loss, the "philanthropist" Browning dismisses her. "He has done more harm than he can ever repair," Alger concluded (LW, 148).

Alger also criticized other forms of market manipulation elsewhere in his juvenile fiction, such as stock watering in *Tom Tracy* (1887) and pyramid-building in *Dan the Newsboy* (1880); in the latter novel, two unscrupulous characters engage "in a hazardous but probably profitable enterprise. It was to procure some genuine certificates of stock in a Western railway for a small number of shares, say five or ten, and raise them ingeniously to fifty and a hundred, and then pledge them as collateral in Wall street for a corresponding sum of money" (DN, 250). Sobered by such blatantly exploitative schemes as these, Alger often expressed the opinion in his late novels that it is better to "be poor and honest . . . than live in a fine house, surrounded by luxury, gained by grinding the faces of the poor" (RA, 143).

Finally, Alger criticized the robber barons for their frequent attempts to break labor strikes. His sympathy for labor seems well documented by his novels. Realizing that wage cuts among rail employees led to the Great Upheaval of 1877, Alger indicated in 1882 that, in his opinion, wage reductions were an "exhibition of meanness" by employers (D&D, 148). Moreover, Alger probably alluded in *A Debt of Honor* (1891) to Gould's successful attempt in 1886 to break the strike called against his rail system by the Knights of Labor. Gould again probably serves as the model for Alger's strike-breaking robber baron, Bradley Wentworth (Gould-Wentworth?). This villain, whose moods are governed solely by "business considerations" (DofH, 175), promises to use his economic clout "to *crush*" any who offend him (DofH, 71).

Perhaps more than any other single characteristic Alger's condemnation of these four business practices evinces the moralistic tone of his juvenile fiction. Far from deserving his modern reputation as an apologist for the robber barons, Alger criticized their dishonesty and, finally, offered prayers for their deliverance. "Wickedness often flourishes in this world," he once wrote. "We must look to the future for compensation" ($500, 63). Unfortunately, Alger himself was not well served by the future, for a generation after his death he had been transformed into a stalking horse for capitalism.

CHAPTER 6

Final Appraisal

I *Reputation*

W HEN Horatio Alger died in 1899, the writer of his brief obituary in *Harper's Weekly* noted that the author "was perhaps better known to the boys of thirty years ago than to the present generation."[1] Available sales statistics tend to substantiate this observation. Certainly the only four best sellers of his long writing career were published between 1868 and 1871,[2] and in 1897 Alger himself estimated his aggregate sales of all volumes at only about 800,000.[3] Sales of the six volumes in the early "Ragged Dick series" contribute a disproportionate share to this total, for Alger also estimated in 1888 that total sales of single books in this series amounted to about 150,000.[4] The reason for his modest popularity in the late nineteenth century would seem to be the charge, leveled frequently by reviewers, parents, ministers, and teachers, that his juvenile fiction was tainted by "sensationalism." For example, a Boston minister in an address at the opening of a branch of the Boston Public Library in 1877 complained about the "endless reams of such drivel poured forth by Horatio Alger, Jr.," and asked "on what principle the managers feel called upon to provide for young and growing minds books which can only weaken and demoralize them."[5] A typical review of an Alger juvenile novel during the Gilded Age indicated that Alger

is always sure of a public, no matter how bad his rhetoric, how unreal his situations, or how crude his workmanship. His latest book, 'Victor Vane, the Young Secretary,' tells, as usual, of the impossible virtues, triumphs and successes of a boy of seventeen, who becomes private secretary and confidential adviser and friend to a Western Congressman, and transacts a large amount of important business in the most experienced fashion. Such stories as this call for little comment. We must recognize the fact that they have taken possession of the mind of the ordinary unreflective boy with

140

a strong hold, and, if possible, supplement this taste for tales of street life with a liking for those that are truly literary.[6]

Strangely, after the author's death there occurred an Alger revival which lasted nearly two decades. In 1910 Alger's juvenile novels were enjoying an *annual* sale of over one million[7]—that is, more of his books were sold each year during the Progressive era than were sold in total during his life—and his books received more favorable comment from reviewers who could sympathize with their moral content if not their literary style. As a reviewer of one Alger reprint suggested in 1906, "If there are no more heroes in grown-up fiction, at least they still exist in young people's stories. Here, for instance, in 'The Young Musician,' is a boy who always does the right thing at the right moment."[8] Alger's books remained popular until the early 1920s and sold an estimated total of between seventeen and twenty million in that period.[9] Thereafter, sales declined rapidly. In 1926, two years before Herbert R. Mayes's debunking biography appeared, the circle of Alger readers had so shrunk[10] that the leading publisher of his books stopped printing them. By 1932, the centenary of Alger's birth, less than twenty per cent of seven thousand surveyed New York boys recognized Alger's name, and only about fourteen per cent admitted to having read even one of his books.[11] In the same year he was described in the pages of *The Literary Digest* as "forgotten."[12] By 1947, a poll of twenty thousand New York children aged eight to fourteen found that ninety-two per cent of those sampled "had never heard of Alger. Less than one per cent had read any of his books."[13]

Still, it is significant that the period of Alger's greatest popularity occurred during the Progressive period of American history when, as Richard Hofstadter has contended, nostalgia for an imagined time of equal opportunity and equitable business practices was intense.[14] Interestingly, at least one edition of *Mark Mason's Triumph* and *Joe's Luck* issued by the New York Book Company during the first decade of the new century has on its cover a picture of President Theodore Roosevelt, although Alger died before the Great Trust-buster assumed the presidency and on no occasion referred to him in his fiction. Alger's most direct successor, Edward Stratemeyer, whose syndicate dominated the juvenile field for over two decades until Stratemeyer's death in 1930, adapted Alger's morality to his own juvenile fiction.[15] Although he changed the formula slightly, as in the Tom Swift series, in general his fiction was a testimony to the endurance of the pattern of moral heroism established by Alger. Two other popular writers of the period who cashed in on the Alger formula, Harold Bell Wright and Gene Stratton-Porter, innovated slightly on the pattern by actually doing what Alger was only accused of doing. Virtuous millionaires and characters who struggle from rags to riches frequent their novels, as in *When a Man's a Man* (1916) and *Michael O'Halloran* (1916). In other words, in their fiction the basic Alger pattern was adopted and slightly modified to suit the materialistic temper of the times, and it seems that Alger, as his own popularity among juveniles waned, was credited with (or blamed for) the innovation. Certainly the clichéd phrase "Horatio Alger hero" entered the popular currency only after Alger himself was rarely read. Indeed, the first appearance in print of that phrase may have occurred as late as 1926, in reference to Alger's old friend Frank A. Munsey,[16] even as Alger's publishers were discontinuing the cheap editions of his books and libraries were removing Alger juveniles from the shelves. That Wright, Porter, and Alger all tapped the same wellsprings of popular sentiment seems apparent from the fact that all were popular during the early years of this century and all had lost that popularity by the eve of the Depression.

The distinction between Alger's modest *fin de siècle* popularity before his death and his period of greatest popularity after his death suggests that there are in effect two Algers—the first a Harvard-educated moralist who expressed his genteel abhorrence of the mercenary Gilded Age, the second a best-selling writer of juvenile stories about poor boys who make good. The first, historical Alger sought a reputation as a teacher and benefactor; the second, distorted, symbolic Alger came to be considered an apologist for industrial capitalism who genuflected at the altar of Success. What accounts for the transformation? The problem, as Malcolm Cowley has stated it, is this: "What I cannot understand is how [Alger] should come to be regarded as the prophet of business enterprise; nor why the family melodrama that he wrote and rewrote for boys should be confused with the American dream of success."[17] While a complete answer to this question—if one is possible—would consume an entire volume of cultural and literary history, three factors instrumental in the transformation can briefly be noted here.

First, the confusion surrounding the publication of the cheap editions of Alger's juveniles early in the twentieth century allowed his moral purpose to be misunderstood. Reprinted in bulk by approximately forty firms between Alger's death and the mid-1920s, the novels consequently were not read in their order of composition during their period of greatest popularity. Indeed, only within the past dozen years, as bibliographers have catalogued Alger's original serializations of the novels and recognized his several pseudonyms, has it been possible to reconstruct the order in which Alger wrote his juvenile books. Because some of Alger's earliest, least mercenary novels were the least reprinted after the turn of the century, a mistaken impression of what Alger did write about was conveyed by the selection of the novels reprinted in cheap editions. And because several of the publishers of cheap Alger juveniles "abridged" some of the books by deleting significant amounts of material, erroneous judgments about the contents of an Alger book were inevitable. The deleted sections often contained descriptions of the hero's charitable activities, never his receipt of his final reward, and thus the moral message of the book was garbled by faulty editing.

A second factor contributing to the distortion of the "first Alger" is that the "second Alger," the mythmaker whose saga of success bears little relation to the books themselves, came into his majority during a period of critical acquiescence. The Alger stories were generally ignored by critics and reviewers even as their popularity soared during the early years of this century. Only the fact of their popularity, not their content, earned the grudging respect of the *literati*. It may be that the success story of the Alger hero was misconstrued during this period at least partly because the modest success of the Alger hero came to be confused with the astounding sales success of the books. If true, this would also account for the persistent, mistaken belief that Horatio Alger was not an author but a character in success stories.

A third factor that contributed to the transformation of Alger into an economic and political symbol was the patriotic fervor of World War II. The process of selective remembering that had begun in the 1920s and 1930s crystallized during the war as Alger became a political shibboleth used in the identification of loyal Americans. The characteristics traditionally (and erroneously) associated with the Horatio Alger hero—the potential greatness of the common man, rugged individualism, economic triumph in a fabled land of opportunity—seemingly summarized the American way of life the war was waged to preserve. In this wartime atmosphere, articles about Alger and his wholesome influence on American youth began appearing for the first time in glossy-paged, mass circulation magazines such as *Esquire, Saturday Review, Time, New Republic,* and the *Atlantic Monthly.* Between November, 1943, and October, 1945, for example, articles about Alger in such mass circulation magazines appeared under the following titles: "A Monument to Free Enterprise," "They Made Me What I Am Today," and "Alger's Vitality."[18] In an apparent attempt to exploit this new interest in Alger during the war, a New York publishing firm in 1945 issued a hardbound reprinting of four Alger novels that had been out of print for a generation, complete with a preface by playwright Russel Crouse. Although the volume was widely reviewed in popular magazines and newspapers, thus reinforcing the popular impression that Alger was enjoying a revival, quite the opposite was the case. Remaindered copies of this 1945 reprinting were available in mint condition as late as 1970, so it would seem that Alger's books were hardly more popular in print than out of print. However, the impression that they were still influential was indelible, and in 1947, soon after the war ended, this Alger-impostor, who was the ideal subject for the publicist, found the best merchandising vehicle for his political and economic wares—the Horatio Alger Awards. Sponsored by the American Schools and Colleges Association, Inc., which had been "concerned about the trend among young people towards the mind-poisoning belief that equal opportunity was a thing of the past," the Alger Awards Committee has honored such men as Bob Hope, Dwight Eisenhower, Ronald Reagan, Billy Graham, W. Clement Stone, and Ray Kroc for meritorious service to the causes of political and religious conservatism and economic orthodoxy.

II *Literary Influence*

Just as the quality of Alger's writing was consistently condemned by critics, the plots of his juvenile novels have been consistently satirized by those authors who have acknowledged it. The critical complaint that Alger was sensational and unrealistic occurred during the same period that two major authors wrote satires of Alger which lampooned his unrealistic "success stories." W. D. Howells, in *The Minister's Charge, or The Apprenticeship of Lemuel Barker* (1887), satirized the country-boy myth which Alger serviced; at issue in this non-comedic satire was the realism of that myth. Stephen Crane in one of his New York Sketches, "A Self-Made Man: An Example of Success That Anyone Can Follow" (1899), apparently parodied Alger's juvenile novel *Tom Tracy*. Crane attempted to lampoon the solemnity of the Alger story by offering a ridiculous version of one. Believing that Alger was his own parodist, Crane simply exaggerated the defects and unbelievable coincidences of the standard Alger plot.

In the twentieth century Alger has been satirized not as an unrealistic writer of guidebooks for the aspiring entrepreneur so much as a popular symbol of success, a symptom of the cultural malaise which afflicts each succeeding generation. The "second Alger," not the first, has been the target of the satirists in this century. F. Scott Fitzgerald, primarily in three works—his play *The Vegetable, or From President to Postman* (1922), the Dan Cody episode in *The Great Gatsby* (1925), and his short story "Forging Ahead" (1929)— parodied Alger the inspiring "mythmaker," the economic symbol. In 1934 Nathanael West parodied Alger in *A Cool Million* by transforming him into a symbol of political repression. More recently, John Seelye in *Dirty Tricks; or, Nick Noxin's Natural Nobility* (1973) further exploited West's premise to offer a political statement about the presidency of Richard Nixon, and Glendon Swarthout in *Luck and Pluck* (1973) chronicled the sexual misadventures of an Algerian anti-hero. William Gaddis in his modernist fiction *JR* (1975), in which an eleven-year-old boy operating out of a telephone booth begins by supplying Navy surplus wooden forks to the Army and ends as the head of a multinational corporation, demonstrated the absurd lengths to which the basic Alger plot could be carried. In other words, the longer Alger's books have remained out of print and unread, the more his basic story has been liable to artistic misappropriation.

In his juvenile books Alger not only influenced those parodists who have been inspired by the creaky machinations of his basic plot, but he also influenced a generation of young readers who grew to adulthood early in this century. To be sure, as one familiar only with Alger's undeserved reputation as an apologist for capitalism might expect, many of these readers—such as Benjamin Fairless of U.S. Steel and James A. Farley of Coca-Cola[19]—became real-life counterparts to the fictional heroes. But to consider Alger simply an apologist for capitalism is to distort grossly his humanitarian purpose. John Cawelti has suggested that "there is as much evidence that Alger was an important influence on future reformers as a popular model for incipient robber barons."[20] As one familiar only with Alger's reputation might *not* expect, many writers on the political left—including Theodore Dreiser, Jack London, Upton Sinclair, and Richard Wright[21]—as youngsters read Alger's books and were not stirred to embrace capitalism. It would seem that either Alger was overrated as an economic and political propagandist or— more probably—his books were simply not designed thematically to spread the gospel of orthodox capitalism and convert the readership of *The Masses*.

Instead, his correspondence and the books themselves reveal that Alger wished simply to be a moral teacher of American youth, carefully instructing them in the traditional virtues of filial piety. That he believed he succeeded in this admittedly limited purpose is clear enough from the fact that he reenacted the same domestic melodrama over a hundred times. Still, he hardly believed that he would be long remembered for this slight achievement, much less celebrated as an American success mythmaker. As he wrote to a friend in 1897, "If I could come back 50 years from now probably I should feel bewildered in reading the New York *Tribune* of 1947."[22] He wrote this with a soothsayer's foresight, for one of the items in the news that year that undoubtedly would have bewildered him beyond his wildest flights of fancy reported the inauguration of the annual Horatio Alger Awards. After fifty years, he could not have recognized his progeny.

Notes and References

Given the number of repositories of Alger's holographs and other biographical material in manuscript, as well as the great number of Alger juvenile titles, some abbreviation has proved necessary. The following code for the location of primary material is used in the notes:

AAS   American Antiquarian Society, Worcester, MA
BYU   Harold B. Lee Library, Brigham Young University
CU   Seligman Papers, Butler Library, Columbia University
HH   Henry E. Huntington Library, San Marino, CA
KC   Seymour Collection, Knox College Archives, Galesburg, IL
HUA   Harvard University Archives, Harvard University
HU   Houghton Library, Harvard University
ISHS   Illinois State Historical Society, Springfield, IL
LC   John Davis Batchelder Autograph Collection, Manuscript Division, Library of Congress
NYPL   Manuscripts and Archives Division, The New York Public Library, Astor, Lenox and Tilden Foundations
SS   Archives, Stratemeyer Syndicate, Maplewood, NJ
SU   Street and Smith Collection, George P. Arents Research Library for Special Collections, Syracuse University
UM   William L. Clements Library, University of Michigan
UV   Horatio Alger Collection, Clifton Waller Barrett Library, University of Virginia Library
YU   Collection of American Literature, Beinecke Rare Book and Manuscript Library, Yale University

The following abbreviations for specific editions of Alger's juvenile books are used in the text and notes. All but four of Alger's juveniles are represented in this list, although many appeared under variant titles. Complete data appears in the notes whenever editions other than these are used.

AC   *Adrift in the City* (Philadelphia, 1895).
ANY   *Adrift in New York*, in *Adrift in New York and The World Before Him* (New York, 1966), pp. 1–144.
ATB   *Adventures of a Telegraph Boy* (New York, 1900).

AG   *Andy Gordon* (Chicago, n.d.).
AGP   *Andy Grant's Pluck* (Chicago, n.d.).
BacB   *The Backwoods Boy* (Philadelphia, n.d.).
BBr   *Ben Bruce* (New York, 1901).
BN   *Ben's Nugget* (Akron, OH, n.d.).
BLB   *Ben the Luggage Boy* (Boston, 1870).
BBA   *Bernard Brooks' Adventures* (New York, 1903).
BB   *Bob Burton* (New York, n.d.).
BR   *Bound to Rise* (New York, 1908).
BF   *A Boy's Fortune* (Philadelphia, 1898).
B&B   *Brave and Bold* (New York, n.d.).
CB   *The Cash Boy* (Chicago, n.d.).
CUB   *Cast Upon the Breakers* (Garden City, NY, 1974).
CCC   *Charlie Codman's Cruise* (Philadelphia, 1894).
CR   *Chester Rand* (Akron, OH, n.d.).
CC   *A Cousin's Conspiracy* (New York, 1909).
DN   *Dan the Newsboy* (New York, n.d.).
DD   *Dean Dunham* (Leyden, MA, 1975).
DofH   *A Debt of Honor* (New York, 1900).
DG   *Digging for Gold: A Story of California* (New York, 1968).
D&D   *Do and Dare* (New York, 1909).
DfH   *Driven from Home* (Chicago, n.d.).
ETB   *The Erie Train Boy* (New York, 1900).
ErB   *The Errand Boy* (New York, 1888).
FW   *Facing the World* (New York, n.d.).
Fa&F   *Fame and Fortune* (Racine, WI, n.d.).
$500   *Five Hundred Dollars* (Chicago, n.d.).
Fr&F   *Frank and Fearless* (Leyden, MA, 1975).
FHP   *Frank Hunter's Peril* (Philadelphia, 1896).
FC   *Frank's Campaign* (Chicago, n.d.).
Canal   *From Canal Boy to President* (New York, 1881).
Farm   *From Farm Boy to Senator* (New York, 1882).
Grit   *Grit* (Akron, OH, n.d.).
HI   *Hector's Inheritance* (Chicago, n.d.).
HH   *Helping Himself* (Chicago, n.d.).
HCL   *Herbert Carter's Legacy* (Chicago, n.d.).
INW   *In a New World* (Akron, OH, n.d.).
IST   *In Search of Treasure* (New York, 1907).
JW   *Jack's Ward* (Chicago, n.d.).
JPB   *Jed the Poorhouse Boy*, in *Struggling Upward and Other Works*
        (New York, 1945), pp. 399–566.
JL   *Joe's Luck* (Akron, OH, n.d.).
Jul   *Julius, in Strive and Succeed: Two Novels by Horatio Alger* (New
        York, 1967).

LL   *Lester's Luck* (Philadelphia, 1901).
L&P   *Luck and Pluck* (Boston, 1869).
LW   *Luke Walton* (New York, n.d.).
MMM   *Mark Manning's Mission* (Leyden, MA, 1975).
MMV   *Mark Mason's Victory* (Chicago, n.d.).
MS   *Mark Stanton* (New York, 1900).
MMB   *Mark the Match Boy*, in *Ragged Dick and Mark the Match Boy* (New York, 1962), pp. 219–382.
NYB   *A New York Boy* (New York, 1901).
OIB   *Only an Irish Boy* (New York, 1910).
PPC   *Paul Prescott's Charge* (Chicago, n.d.).
PP   *Paul the Peddler* (Chicago, n.d.).
PF   *Phil the Fiddler*, in *Struggling Upward and Other Works* (New York, 1945), pp. 281–398.
RD   *Ragged Dick*, in *Ragged Dick and Mark the Match Boy* (New York, 1962), pp. 39–216.
RRH   *Ralph Raymond's Heir* (Chicago, n.d.).
RfR   *Risen from the Ranks* (New York, 1910).
RCS   *Robert Coverdale's Struggle* (New York, n.d.).
RS   *A Rolling Stone* (Leyden, MA, 1975).
Ro&R   *Rough and Ready* (Boston, 1869).
Ru&R   *Rufus and Rose* (Boston, 1870).
RA   *Rupert's Ambition* (Philadelphia, 1899).
SC   *Sam's Chance* (Chicago, n.d.).
SH   *Shifting for Himself* (Racine, WI, n.d.).
SSOB   *Silas Snobden's Office Boy* (Garden City, NY, 1973).
SorS   *Sink or Swim* (Chicago, n.d.).
Sl&S   *Slow and Sure* (Chicago, n.d.).
StB   *The Store Boy*, in *Strive and Succeed: Two Novels by Horatio Alger* (New York, 1967).
St&Su   *Strive and Succeed* (New York, 1909).
St&St   *Strong and Steady* (Boston, 1871).
SU   *Struggling Upward*, in *Struggling Upward and Other Works* (New York, 1945), pp. 3–148.
TT   *Tattered Tom* (Boston, 1871).
TelB   *The Telegraph Boy* (Chicago, n.d.).
TinB   *The Tin Box* (New York, n.d.).
TBr   *Tom Brace* (Philadelphia, n.d.).
TTC   *Tom Temple's Career* (Racine, WI, n.d.).
TTF   *Tom Thatcher's Fortune* (New York, 1888).
TomB   *Tom the Bootblack* (New York, n.d.).
TTr   *Tom Tracy* (New York, 1900).
TTL   *Tom Turner's Legacy* (New York, 1902).
TrB   *The Train Boy* (Akron, OH, n.d.).

T&T   *Try and Trust* (Racine, WI, n.d.).
VV   *Victor Vane* (Philadelphia, 1894).
W&H   *Wait and Hope* (New York, 1909).
W&W   *Wait and Win* (New York, 1908).
WG   *Walter Griffith* (New York, 1901).
WSP   *Walter Sherwood's Probation* (Chicago, n.d.).
WBH   *The World Before Him*, in *Adrift in New York and The World Before Him* (New York, 1966), pp. 145–302.
YAc   *The Young Acrobat* (Chicago, n.d.).
YAd   *The Young Adventurer* (New York, n.d.).
YCR   *The Young Circus Rider* (Philadelphia, 1883).
YEx   *The Young Explorer* (Chicago, n.d.).
YMin   *The Young Miner* (Chicago, n.d.).
YMus   *The Young Musician* (New York, n.d.).
YO   *The Young Outlaw* (New York, n.d.).
YS   *The Young Salesman* (Chicago, n.d.).

Preface

1. Samuel Eliot Morison and Henry Steele Commager, *The Growth of the American Republic*, 2nd ed. (New York, 1937), pp. 287–88.
2. Frederick Lewis Allen, *The Big Change* (New York, 1952), p. 56.
3. Kenneth S. Lynn, *The Dream of Success* (Boston, 1955), p. 6.

Chapter One

1. Both the date and year of Alger's birth have been the subject of some dispute, but the two most reliable sources, Alger's handwritten autobiographical sketch in the Harvard University Archives and Arthur M. Alger, *A Genealogical History of That Branch of the Alger Family Which Springs from Thomas Alger of Taunton and Bridgewater, in Massachusetts 1665–1875* (Boston, 1876), pp. 45–46, agree on this date and year. Except where otherwise indicated, the data about Alger's family are found in this genealogical history.
2. See, for example, the senior Alger's article, "The Prophecies of the Old Testament Respecting the Messiah," *Monthly Religious Magazine and Theological Review*, VIII (April 1851), 167–76. Previous biographers have characterized the senior Alger as a tyrannical parent who insisted that his namesake also enter the ministry. No available evidence confirms this. Indeed, the junior Alger dedicated *Fame and Fortune* (1868) to his father, "from whom I have never failed to receive literary sympathy and encouragement."
3. Edward F. Hayward, *History of the Second Parish Church (Unitarian)* (Marlborough, MA, 1906), pp. 19–21.

4. Benjamin Shurtleff, *The History of the Town of Revere* (Boston, 1938), *passim*.

5. Reform movements have been depicted as instruments of social control in the hands of a displaced elite by Joseph R. Gusfield, *Symbolic Crusade* (Urbana, IL, 1963), esp. pp. 36–60; and David Donald, *Lincoln Reconsidered*, 2nd ed. (New York, 1961), pp. 19–36.

6. Class Book of 1852, HUA MSS.

7. Alger grew to a height of only five feet, two inches, and suffered respiratory illnesses throughout his life, according to Grace Williamson Edes, *Annals of the Harvard Class of 1852* (Cambridge, MA, 1922), p. 5. Edes gleaned her data from letters Alger wrote to Henry Denny, her grandfather and secretary of the Harvard class.

8. See David Riesman et al., *The Lonely Crowd* (New Haven, CT, 1961), pp. 99–104.

9. Class Book of 1852, HUA MSS.; Alger to Irving Blake, 12 November 1898, HH MSS.

10. Edes, p. 6.

11. "Horatio Alger, Jr.," *Golden Argosy*, 17 October 1885, p. 364. This biographical sketch, which Alger himself recommended to Barton A. Aylesworth, president of Drake University (12 November 1894, BYU MSS.), is an especially valuable source because its contents were apparently supplied by Alger, and it is virtually the only published article of its kind to appear during Alger's life.

12. Edes, p. 6; *Historical Register of Harvard University 1636–1936* (Cambridge, MA, 1937), p. 77.

13. HUA.

14. Alger to Henry Wadsworth Longfellow, 16 December 1875, HU MSS. Quoted by permission of the Houghton Library.

15. Alger to James Fenimore Cooper, 12 September 1850, YU MSS.

16. Harvard College catalogue for the class of 1852, pp. 42–44.

17. Daniel W. Howe, *The Unitarian Conscience: Harvard Moral Philosophy 1805–1861* (Cambridge, MA, 1970), p. 27.

18. Howe, p. 69.

19. Joseph Butler, *Analogy of Religion* (New York, 1870), p. 329.

20. Thomas Reid, *Essays on the Intellectual Powers of Man,* (Cambridge, MA, 1969), p. 724.

21. Howe, p. 232.

22. Class Book of 1852, HUA MSS.

23. Edes, p. 6. Unless otherwise indicated, all biographical data in this paragraph are found in Edes's volume or annotations in the Class Book of 1852, hereafter cited as HUA.

24. For example, Alger's religious poem "A Chant of Life" appeared in the Boston *Evening Transcript* for 11 April 1853.

25. A. M. Alger, p. 46; Alger to Blake, 28 April 1896, HH MSS.

26. Horatio Alger, Jr., "Writing Stories for Boys," *The Writer*, IX (February 1896), 36.

27. Although it must be used with caution, the best bibliographical source about Alger's short works appears in the December, 1974, issue of *Newsboy*, the publication of the Horatio Alger Society.

28. Frank M. O'Brien, *The Story of the Sun, New York 1833–1928* (New York, 1928), pp. 141–42.

29. A. M. Alger, p. 46; Alger to Blake, 16 November 1896, HH MSS; Alger to ?, 2 January 1869, UV MSS.

30. Alger to William Conant Church, 23 April 1866, NYPL MSS.

31. "An Affair of Honor," *Harper's Monthly*, XVIII (December 1858), 43–46, is attributed to Alger by the *Index* to *Harper's Monthly* volumes I–XXV; "Barbara's Courtship," later reprinted in Alger's *Grand'ther Baldwin's Thanksgiving* (Boston, 1875), originally appeared in *Harper's Monthly*, XIV (April 1857), 658.

32. Horatio Alger to Ralph Waldo Emerson, 28 December 1853, HU MSS. The senior Alger eventually represented Marlborough in the state legislature (Marlborough *Mirror*, 18 February 1860).

33. Alger, Jr., to Blake, 18 December 1896, HH MSS.

34. Edes, p. 7. Unless otherwise indicated, all biographical data in this paragraph are found in Edes's volume or HUA.

35. Horatio Alger, Jr., "A Visit to the Home of Walter Scott," *Golden Argosy*, 14 April 1883; Alger to Blake, 10 July 1896, HH MSS.

36. "Eugene Scribe," *North American Review*, XCVII (October 1863), 325–38. Alger's authorship of this essay is corroborated by *Poole's Index*.

37. HUA.

38. *Supplement to the Cyclopedia of American Literature*, ed. Evert A. Duyckinck and George L. Duyckinck (New York, 1866), p. 145.

39. Alger to Edwin R. A. Seligman, 14 July 1885, CU MSS. Grant himself failed to mention this fact, interestingly enough, in his autobiography *Fourscore* (1934).

40. HUA.

41. Letters of Dean to his mother in the Boston Public Library frequently mention Alger.

42. A complete discussion of contributions by Alger to *Frank Leslie's Illustrated Newspaper* appears in the January-February, 1977, issue of *Newsboy*.

43. Alger to William Conant Church, 20 April 1866, NYPL MSS.

44. The original appearances of most of these Civil War poems in such newspapers as the New York *Evening Post* and New York *Ledger* have not been discovered; however, they were reprinted in Alger's *Grand'ther Baldwin's Thanksgiving* (1875). See holograph of "Carving a Name" (NYPL MSS) and Frederick J. Shepard, "A Wandering Legend of Lake Erie," Buffalo *Evening News*, 16 July 1927, magazine section, p. 9.

45. HUA.

46. *Life and Letters of Edward Everett Hale*, ed. Edward Everett Hale, Jr. (Boston, 1917), pp. 366–67.

47. "Writing Stories for Boys," p. 36.

48. Alger to E. C. Stedman, 29 November 1875, YU MSS. Alger also enclosed a review of Stedman's *Victorian Poets* from the Boston *Christian Register*, and asked him for Bayard Taylor's address so that he might "send him my little book." On 9 January 1888, Alger wrote Stedman again, enclosing samples of poetry written by his student Elizabeth Cardozo, to solicit his estimate of their worth (NYPL MSS).

49. "Horatio Alger, Jr.," p. 364.

50. Archives of the First Unitarian Church of Brewster, Massachusetts.

51. Alger to W. S. Sargent, 14 October 1884, KC MSS.

52. Alger to Reverend George Chaney, 25 November 1864, HU MSS. Although Alger and Hale apparently were intimate at this time, no record of a further exchange is known to exist. In other words, the subsequent "Brewster affair" and Alger's defrocking may have led to the end of their friendship.

53. Alger to Evert A. Duyckinck, 28 January 1866, NYPL MSS.

54. Archives of the First Unitarian Church of Brewster, Massachusetts. Excerpts from these church records have appeared previously in Richard M. Huber, *The American Idea of Success* (New York, 1971), pp. 45–46, and in Edwin P. Hoyt, *Horatio's Boys* (Radnor, PA, 1974), pp. 5–6.

55. Alger to ?, 2 January 1869, UV MSS.

56. Alger to Blake, 10 July 1896, HH MSS.

57. Alger to William Conant Church, 20 April 1866, NYPL MSS.

58. Although composed and submitted in 1866, this poem did not reach print until 1872 in the *New York Weekly*.

59. Howe, p. 195.

60. Ibid. pp. 192–93.

61. "Writing Stories for Boys," p. 37.

Chapter Two

1. "Horatio Alger, Jr.," p. 364.

2. This information is provided by Alger enthusiast Gilbert K. Westgard II of Des Plaines, IL. It is also mentioned in Hoyt, p. 4.

3. Horatio Alger, Jr., "How I Came to Write 'John Maynard,'" *The Writer*, VIII (December 1895), 182–83.

4. "Horatio Alger, Jr.," p. 364.

5. Alger to Duyckinck, 28 January 1866, NYPL MSS; Alger to Blake, 21 March 1898, HH MSS.

6. Horatio Alger, Jr., *Ragged Dick* (Boston, 1868), pp. vii–viii. There is no evidence that Alger knew Charles Loring Brace personally or fre-

quented the Newsboys' Lodging House for years, contrary to previous claims, although his name does appear on a list of donors to the Society during fiscal year 1873 (*Twenty-first Annual Report of the Children's Aid Society* [New York, 1873]).

7. "Horatio Alger, Jr.," p. 364.

8. Horatio Alger, Jr., *Fame and Fortune* (Boston, 1868), p. viii.

9. HUA.

10. George S. Hellman, *Benjamin N. Cardozo: American Judge* (New York, 1940), p. 14.

11. Gary Scharnhorst, "A Note on the Authorship of Alger's *Life of Edwin Forrest*," *Theatre Studies*, XXIII (1976–77), 53–55.

12. "Harvard Club Dinner," *New York Times*, 24 February 1869, p. 8, col. 2.

13. HUA.

14. A. M. Alger, pp. 43–45.

15. Horatio Alger, Jr. to William Rounseville Alger, 7 December 1874, YU MSS; H. Alger to Seligman, 9 November 1876, CU MSS.

16. Edward S. Martin, *The Life of Joseph Hodges Choate* (New York, 1920), p. 319.

17. Quoted in Henry James, *Autobiography*, ed. Frederick W. Dupee (New York, 1956), p. 401.

18. James, p. 401.

19. "Horatio Alger, Jr.," p. 364.

20. Ibid.

21. Ibid.; also Edes, p. 10; BR, v–vi; Alger, "A Glimpse of Venice," *Young Israel*, IV (January 1874); "A Visit to the Home of Walter Scott," *Golden Argosy*, 14 April 1883; Alger to Blake, 10 July 1896, HH MSS. Two poems which originally appeared in *Grand'ther Baldwin's Thanksgiving* (1875), "In the Church at Stratford-on-Avon" and "Mrs. Browning's Grave at Florence," also indicate sites the party visited.

22. "Writing Stories for Boys," pp. 36–37.

23. See, for example, the review in *The Nation*, 1 June 1876, p. 354.

24. Alger to Stedman, 9 January 1888, NYPL MSS. Stedman received his copy of the volume as a gift through a mutual friend, Alexander Henriques, the vice-chairman of the New York Stock Exchange.

25. Alger to Henry Denny, 6 March 1893, HUA MSS.

26. Alger to Seligman, 6 August 1877, CU MSS.

27. Alger to Seligman, 3 January 1878, 15 July 1878, CU MSS.

28. "Horatio Alger, Jr.," p. 364; Alger to Blake, 10 July 1896, HH MSS.

29. Alger to Seligman, 15 February 1877, CU MSS.

30. Alger to Seligman, 21 February 1877, 13 March 1877, CU MSS.

31. Alger to Seligman, 7 May 1877, CU MSS.

32. Portland *Oregonian*, 4 May 1877, p. 3, col. 2.

33. Alger to Seligman, 1 April 1878, CU MSS.

34. Horatio Alger, Jr., "Are My Boys Real?," *Ladies' Home Journal*, VII (November 1890), 29. This article has been reprinted in the January–February, 1975, issue of *Newsboy*.

35. Josiah Lightheart, "Ragged Dick/The Author, Horatio Alger Jr., a Visitor in This City," San Francisco *Daily Morning Call*, a November 1890, p. 12; "Passengers for Portland," Portland *Oregonian*, 30 October 1890, p. 6, col. 6.

36. Alger to Blake, 2 June 1896, HH MSS.

37. Alger to Seligman, 6 August 1877, 15 July 1878, CU MSS; Alger to Mr. Elderkin, 2 August 1884, YU MSS; Alger to Blake, 7 August 1894, HH MSS; *The Critic*, 27 July 1895, p. 61.

38. Alger to Seligman, 15 July 1878, CU MSS.

39. Alger to Seligman, 5 September 1879, CU MSS.

40. Quoted in Drew Pearson and Robert S. Allen, *The Nine Old Men* (Garden City, NY, 1936), p. 215.

41. Harvard College catalogue for the class of 1852, p. 42.

42. Quoted in Howe, p. 228.

43. Alger to Lee & Shepard, 15 November 1872, AAS MSS.

44. Alger to Seligman, 15 November 1877, CU MSS.

45. Alger to Seligman, 14 November (1885?), CU MSS.

46. Harvard College catalogue for the class of 1852, p. 42.

47. Alger to Seligman, 9 November 1876, CU MSS.

48. Horatio Alger to Russell A. Alger, 28 June 1888, 4 July 1888, UM MSS; H. Alger to Blake, 26 June 1896, 7 November 1897, HH MSS.

49. Alger to Blake, 9 September 1896, HH MSS.

50. Quentin Reynolds, *The Fiction Factory* (New York, 1955), pp. 83–85; George Britt, *Forty Years—Forty Millions* (New York, 1935), pp. 56, 61, 92. Frank Stockton wrote Alger in 1873 to solicit submissions to the prestigious juvenile magazine *St. Nicholas*, but Alger's contract with Street forbade him from writing for a competitor (William W. Ellsworth, *A Golden Age of Authors* [Boston and New York, 1919], p. 92).

51. Alger to Blake, 23 December 1896, HH MSS.

52. Alger to Blake, 2 August 1895, HH MSS; Alger to Edward Stratemeyer, 18 November 1898, SS MSS.

53. "Crimson to the Fore," *New York Times*, 20 February 1892, p. 3, col. 1; Edes, p. 11.

54. Alger to Seligman, 1 July 1885, CU MSS.

55. Alger to Blake, 26 October 1896, 3 December 1896, HH MSS.

56. Alger to Blake, 28 April 1896, HH MSS.

57. Alger to Blake, 12 May 1897, HH MSS; LL, 249.

58. Alger to A. B. Paine, 16 October 1895, HH MSS.

59. Alger to Blake, 7 October 1894, 18 September 1895, 27 July 1896, HH MSS.

60. Manuscript copies of this poem are housed in the NYPL and UV.

61. Alger to Stedman, 29 November 1875, YU MSS; see BacB, 117.

62. The book catalogues of the G. W. Dillingham publishing firm list Alger's name as the author of this book as early as 1900. One of the characters in the novel, significantly, is named Irving Blake after Alger's friend and correspondent.

63. Alger to Victor H. Wolff, 23 July 1879, ISHS MSS; Alger to Barton A. Aylesworth, 12 November 1894, BYU MSS; Alger to Seligman, 6 August 1877, CU MSS.

64. Alger to Blake, 5 February 1896, 26 October 1896, HH MSS.

65. H. Alger to R. A. Alger, 2 May 1888, UM MSS; "Horatio Alger, Jr.," p. 364.

66. H. Alger to R. A. Alger, 10 November 1898, UM MSS.

67. Alger to Blake, 1 January 1898, HH MSS.

68. H. Alger to R. A. Alger, 10 November 1898, UM MSS.

69. Alger to Blake, 4 April 1895, HH MSS.

70. Alger to Blake, 3 January 1896, HH MSS.

71. Alger to Stratemeyer, 18 December 1898, SS MSS. Incredibly, Frank Gruber in *Horatio Alger, Jr.* (West Los Angeles, 1961), p. 39, claims that Alger's annual income may be conservatively estimated at $20,000 during these years.

72. Alger to Stratemeyer, 18 December 1898, SS MSS.

73. Ibid.

74. See, for example, Alger's obituaries in the *New York Times,* 19 July 1899, p. 7, col. 5, and in the Chicago *Daily Tribune,* 19 July 1899, p. 2, col. 6.

75. Alger to Blake, 16 February 1897, HH MSS.

76. A copy of Alger's probated will was provided by Alger collector Bob Bennett of Mt. Pleasant, MI.

77. Frank A. Munsey, *The Founding of the Munsey Publishing-House* (New York, 1907), p. 6.

Chapter Three

1. Howe, pp. 188, 190.

2. Quoted in Howe, p. 190.

3. Bruce E. Coad, "The Alger Hero," in *Heroes of Popular Culture,* ed. Ray B. Browne et al. (Bowling Green, OH, 1972), p. 44.

4. Moses Rischin, *The American Gospel of Success* (Chicago, 1965), p. 21. See also Lynn, *The Dream of Success,* p. 7.

5. See especially John Cawelti, *Apostles of the Self-Made Man* (Chicago, 1965), pp. 108–120; and Rychard Fink, "Horatio Alger as a Social Philosopher," intro. to *Ragged Dick and Mark the Match Boy* by Horatio Alger (New York, 1962), pp. 27–30.

6. Horatio Alger, Jr., "Beauty versus Money," *Gleason's Weekly Line-of-Battle Ship*, 12 February 1859, p. 7.

7. Between 1857 and 1860, while a student at Cambridge Divinity School, Alger published a total of eight novelle in the New York *Sun* newspaper. The titles of these stories and their dates of publication are as follows: "Hugo, the Deformed," 27 January to 7 February 1857; "Madeline, the Temptress," 7 August to 4 September 1857; "The Secret Drawer, or the Story of a Missing Will," 14 June to 5 July 1859; "The Cooper's Ward, or the Waif of the New Year," 8 December 1858 to 10 January 1859; "Herbert Selden, the Poor Lawyer's Son," 5 March to 12 April 1859; "Manson the Miser, or Life and Its Vicissitudes," 18 May to 21 June 1859; "The Gipsy Nurse, or Marked for Life," 15 August to 14 September 1859; and "The Discarded Son," 3 February to 2 March 1860. Although these works were written according to the formula of popular sentimental romance, by all indications they attracted slight popular attention. "Manson the Miser" was slightly rewritten for a juvenile audience and published in 1866 under the title *Charlie Codman's Cruise (Newsboy*, XII [August 1973], pp. 8–9; letter from Gilbert K. Westgard II to Scharnhorst, 12 July 1974).

After printing this series of eight novelle cut from the same sentimental fabric, the *Sun* editors rejected further adult works from Alger's pen. "Marie Bertrand," his ninth adult novel, set in Paris and at least partially autobiographical, was finally serialized in the *New York Weekly* in 1864. For a brief plot summary, see Ralph D. Gardner, *Horatio Alger, or The American Hero Era* (Mendota, IL, 1964), pp. 437–38. "Marie Bertrand" is a precursor of Alger's urban novels which employ a guidebook description of a city—in this case Paris rather than New York or Chicago.

Alger's tenth and eleventh adult novels, both of which were published by Loring of Boston in 1866, were a revision of "The Cooper's Ward" retitled *Timothy Crump's Ward* and a revision of "The Discarded Son" retitled *Helen Ford*. For plot summaries, see John Tebbel, *From Rags to Riches* (New York, 1963), pp. 168–93. *Timothy Crump's Ward* was later rewritten for a juvenile audience and published, in 1875, under the title *Jack's Ward*.

Alger's twelfth attempt to write a substantial adult work, "Ralph Raymond's Heir," was serialized in *Gleason's Literary Companion* in 1869 and, slightly rewritten, appeared as a juvenile novel in 1892 under the same title.

8. Horatio Alger, Jr., *Helen Ford* (Boston, 1866), p. 297.

9. *Helen Ford*, pp. 262, 265.

10. "Hugo, the Deformed," New York *Sun*, 7 February 1857; rpt. in *Newsboy*, XII (December 1973), 20.

11. "Manson the Miser," New York *Sun*, 21 June 1859.

12. For plot summaries of three of these stories, see Tebbel, pp. 145–52.

13. "Love," *Putnam's*, O.S. IX (March 1857), 235–43.

14. "Five Hundred Dollars," *Graham's Illustrated Magazine*, LII (January 1858), 30–32.

15. "Farmer Hayden's Thanksgiving-Day," *Harper's Weekly*, 5 December 1863, pp. 774–75. The authorship of this unsigned story, like that of "Love" in note 13 above, may be attributed to Alger on the basis of internal and external evidence.

16. "Job Warner's Christmas," *Harper's Monthly*, XXVIII (December 1863), 119–24.

17. "Ralph Farnham's Romance," *Harper's Monthly*, XXVIII (March 1864), 500–507.

18. *The New Schoolma'am; or, A Summer in North Sparta* (Boston, 1877). Slightly rewritten, this novel was reprinted under the title "A Fancy of Hers" in *Munsey's Magazine*, VI (March 1892), 697–744; rpt. in *Newsboy*, XIII (March–April 1975), 7–31. Subsequent references in the text to this work, indicated parenthetically, are to the original printing.

19. Quoted in Henry F. May, *Protestant Churches and Industrial America* (New York, 1949), p. 94.

20. The only previous mention in print of this manuscript appears in Gardner, p. 436. Gardner merely reported its existence, however, and had not read it. Edward Stratemeyer, the creator of the Rover Boys series, used the MS to "complete" a juvenile novel, entitled *Jerry the Backwoods Boy*, which he published in 1904 under Alger's name. However, the unrevised MS is the only authentic adult version of this novel.

21. On 15 July 1878, Alger wrote to E. R. A. Seligman that "I have completed a new novel, nearly half as long again as the 'New Schoolma'am.' I am not sure that it will be published this year. The book-trade is dull, and I prefer to delay it, rather than have it a comparative failure. I shall limit the decision to the publisher" (CU MSS). This "new novel" is "Mabel Parker." Not only is the MS about "half as long again" as *The New Schoolma'am*, but Alger mentioned Francis S. Street, his publisher, in the same letter. The MS is owned by the Street and Smith Collection at Syracuse University.

22. Similarities between the works, in addition to setting, include an archery match reminiscent of Leatherstocking's turkey shoot, the simultaneous shooting of a deer by two characters and their ensuing argument, and parallel characterizations, notably Mabel and Henry with Elizabeth Temple and Edward Effingham.

23. See Leslie Fiedler, *Love and Death in the American Novel*, 2nd ed. (New York, 1966), pp. 209–87.

24. Horatio Alger, Jr., "Mabel Parker; or, The Hidden Treasure. A Tale of the Frontier Settlements," unpublished novel, c. 1878, p. 57 (SU MSS). Quoted by permission of The Condé Nast Publications Inc. Subsequent references to the text of the MS are supplied parenthetically.

25. Julian Starr [Horatio Alger, Jr.], *The Disagreeable Woman: A Social Mystery* (New York, 1895); rpt. in *Newsboy*, XIII (October–November 1974), 1, 8–28. Subsequent references in the text to this work, indicated parenthetically, are to the later, more accessible printing.

26. William Lawrence, "The Relation of Wealth to Morals," *World's Work*, I (1901), 286–87.

Chapter Four

1. Alger to Mr. Elderkin, 2 August 1884, YU MSS; Canal, 6.

2. "Advice from Horatio Alger, Jr.," *The Writer*, VI (January 1892), 16.

3. Alger to C. T. Scott, 25 March 1895, LC MSS.

4. "Writing Stories for Boys," p. 37.

5. *Fame and Fortune* (Boston, 1868), p. viii.

6. Benjamin Franklin, *Autobiography and Other Writings*, ed. by Russel B. Nye (Boston, 1958), pp. 26–27.

7. Cawelti, p. 118.

8. Louis B. Wright, "Franklin's Legacy to the Gilded Age," *Virginia Quarterly Review*, XXII (1946), 279.

9. Tebbel, p. 11.

10. Forty years before the Melville revival of the 1920s, Alger recommended "the fascinating narratives of Herman Melville" to his readers (Canal, 23–24).

11. Cawelti, p. 110.

12. Howe, p. 67.

13. Howe, p. 159.

14. Howe, p. 64.

15. Howe, p. 67.

16. Stewart Holbrook, *Lost Men of American History* (New York, 1946), p. 228.

17. Russel B. Nye, *Society and Culture in America: 1830–1860* (New York, 1974), pp. 334–36.

18. Howe, p. 140.

19. Thorstein Veblen, *The Theory of the Leisure Class* (New York, 1934), p. 70.

20. Howe, pp. 241–42.

21. Howe, p. 111.

22. Dugald Stewart, *The Philosophy of the Active and Moral Powers of Man,* ed. Sir William Hamilton (Boston, 1855), I, 101.

23. Howe, p. 229.

24. *Ragged Dick* (Boston, 1868), p. vii; Alger, *Mark the Match Boy* (Boston, 1869), p. vii–viii.

25. Herbert R. Mayes, *Alger: A Biography Without a Hero* (New York, 1928), p. 145.

26. Alger, *The Telegraph Boy* (Boston, 1879), p. vii.
27. Alger, *Ben's Nugget* (Philadelphia, 1882), p. 7.
28. Stewart, I, p. 188.
29. Howe, p. 239.
30. Howe, p. 255.

Chapter Five

1. Alger, "A. T. Stewart," *Golden Argosy*, 10 March 1883.
2. C. Wright Mills, "The American Business Elite: A Collective Portrait," *The Tasks of Economic History* (suppl. issue of *Journal of Economic History*), V (1945), 20–44.
3. Cawelti, p. 119.
4. Michael Zuckerman, "The Nursery Tales of Horatio Alger," *American Quarterly*, XXIV (May 1972), 193.
5. Richard Weiss, *The Myth of American Success* (New York, 1969), pp. 49, 59–60.
6. Cawelti, p. 120.
7. Unfortunately, this crucial fact is too little appreciated. Most editors of Alger's novels after the turn of the century deliberately tried to deemphasize their antebellum setting by changing all dates. Thus in the original edition of *Tony the Tramp* (1876), for example, the hero writes a letter dated 1857; the same letter is dated 1887 in the twentieth-century reprinting.
8. Blanche Evans Hazard, *The Organization of the Boot and Shoe Industry in Massachusetts Before 1875* (Cambridge, MA, 1921), p. 6.
9. Hazard, p. 98.
10. Howe, p. 126.
11. John P. Sisk, "Rags to Riches: Horatio Alger and the Age of the Robber Barons," *Commonweal*, 3 January 1958, p. 352.
12. Howe, p. 143.
13. Zuckerman, p. 204.
14. Matthew Josephson, *The Robber Barons* (New York, 1934), p. 198.

Chapter Six

1. E. S. Martin, "This Busy World," *Harper's Weekly*, 5 August 1899, p. 761.
2. Frank Luther Mott, *Golden Multitudes* (New York, 1947), pp. 309, 321, 322.
3. *Who's Who in America 1899–1900*, ed. John W. Leonard (Chicago, 1899), p. 10. In a letter to Blake (25 March 1897, HH MSS) Alger mentioned the receipt of the information form to be completed for this volume.
4. Horatio Alger, Jr. to R. A. Alger, 2 May 1888, UM MSS.

5. "Literary Rubbish," *Library Journal*, II (1878), 299.

6. "New Books and New Editions," *The Critic*, 29 June 1895, p. 476.

7. Everett T. Tomlinson, "The Perpetual 'Best-Sellers,'" *World's Work*, XX (June 1910), p. 13045.

8. "Found: A Hero," *New York Times Saturday Review of Books*, 8 December 1906, p. 846.

9. Mott, p. 159.

10. Arthur M. Jordan, *Children's Interests in Reading* (Chapel Hill, NC, 1926), *passim*.

11. "The Cynical Youngest Generation," *The Nation*, 17 February 1932, p. 186.

12. "A Forgotten Boy's Classic," *Literary Digest*, 30 January 1932, p. 20.

13. "Horatio Alger is an Unknown to 92% of Boys and Girls in Seven Clubs in City," *New York Times*, 13 January 1947, p. 23, col. 2–3.

14. Richard Hofstadter, *The Age of Reform* (New York, 1955), pp. 131–73.

15. Russel B. Nye, *The Unembarrassed Muse* (New York, 1970), p. 76.

16. "Frank A. Munsey as a Horatio Alger Hero," *Literary Digest*, 9 January 1926, p. 48.

17. Malcolm Cowley, "Horatio Alger: Failure," *Horizon*, XII (Summer 1970), 65.

18. *Saturday Review*, 1 September 1945, pp. 15–16; *Atlantic Monthly*, CLXXII (November 1943), 115–17; *New Republic*, 1 October 1945, p. 441.

19. Ralph D. Gardner, "Foreword" to *Silas Snobden's Office Boy* by Horatio Alger, Jr. (Garden City, NY, 1973), p. 12.

20. Cawelti, p. 117.

21. Theodore Dreiser, *Dawn* (New York, 1931), p. 122; Jack London, *John Barleycorn* (New York, 1913), p. 133; Upton Sinclair, *Autobiography* (New York, 1962), p. 9; Jay Martin, *Nathanael West* (New York, 1970), p. 235; Richard Wright, "Alger Revisited, or My Stars! Did We Read That Stuff?," *PM*, 16 September 1945, magazine section, p. 13.

22. Alger to Blake, 12 May 1897, HH MSS.

Selected Bibliography

PRIMARY SOURCES

A fuller list of Alger titles occurs at the beginning of the Notes and References section. The list below is limited to modern and more accessible editions of many of those works.

Adrift in New York and The World Before Him. Ed. William Coyle. New York: Odyssey Press, 1966.
Alger Street: The Collected Poetry of Horatio Alger, Jr. Ed. Gilbert K. Westgard II. Boston: Canner, 1964.
Cast Upon the Breakers. Foreword by Ralph D. Gardner. Garden City: Doubleday & Co., 1974.
Dean Dunham; or, the Waterford Mystery. Leyden, MA: Aeonian Press, 1974.
Digging for Gold: A Story of California. Introduction by John Seelye. New York: Collier, 1968.
The Erie Train Boy. Leyden, MA: Aeonian Press, 1974.
Frank and Fearless; or, the Fortunes of Jasper Kent. Leyden, MA: Aeonian Press, 1974.
From Canal Boy to President; or, the Boyhood and Manhood of James A. Garfield. New York: Scholarly Reprints, 1976.
In a New World. New York: Media, 1972.
Making His Way: Frank Courtney's Struggle Upward. New York: Arno, 1975.
Mark Manning's Mission; or, the Story of a Shoe Factory Boy. Leyden, MA: Aeonian Press, 1974.
Phil, the Fiddler; or, the Young Street Musician. North Plainfield, NJ: Galloway, 1971.
Ragged Dick and Mark the Match Boy. Introduction by Rychard Fink. New York: Collier, 1962.
Ralph Raymond's Heir. Leyden, MA: Aeonian Press, 1974.
Risen from the Ranks. New York: Media, 1972.
A Rolling Stone; or, the Adventures of a Wanderer. Leyden, MA: Aeonian Press, 1974.

Silas Snobden's Office Boy. Foreword by Ralph D. Gardner. Garden City: Doubleday & Co., 1973.

Strive and Succeed: Two Novels by Horatio Alger. Introduction by S. N. Behrman. New York: Holt, Rinehart and Winston, 1967.

Strong and Steady, or, Paddle Your Own Canoe. Canoga Park, CA: Major Books, 1975.

Struggling Upward and Other Works. Preface by Russel Crouse. New York: Bonanza Books, 1945.

The Young Miner; or, Tom Nelson in California. Introduction by John Seeyle. San Francisco: The Book Club of California, 1965.

The Young Outlaw; or, Adrift in the Streets. Canoga Park, CA: Major Books, 1975.

SECONDARY SOURCES

A. Biography

Gardner, Ralph D. *Horatio Alger, or The American Hero Era.* Mendota, IL: Wayside Press, 1964. Contrived to entertain book collectors but unfortunately accepted as authoritative.

Gruber, Frank. *Horatio Alger, Jr.: A Biography and a Bibliography.* West Los Angeles: Grover Jones Press, 1961. Superficial and incomplete, but generally accurate.

Hoyt, Edwin P. *Horatio's Boys: The Life and Works of Horatio Alger, Jr.* Radnor, PA: Chilton Book Co., 1974. Flawed by reliance on Gardner and sensational details about Alger's alleged homosexuality.

Mayes, Herbert R. *Alger: A Biography Without a Hero.* New York: Macy-Masius, 1928. An admitted hoax that succeeded for over forty years.

Tebbel, John. *From Rags to Riches: Horatio Alger and the American Dream.* New York: Macmillan, 1963. Deeply flawed by heavy reliance on Mayes's biography.

B. Criticism

Beck, Warren. *"Huckleberry Finn* versus *The Cash Boy." Education,* XLIX (September 1928), 1–13. Contains valuable comments on Alger's style.

Cawelti, John G. *Apostles of the Self-Made Man: Changing Concepts of Success in America.* Chicago: U. of Chicago Press, 1965. Devotes an entire chapter to Alger's "rags to respectability" theme. Valuable scholarly assessment.

———. "Portrait of the Newsboy as a Young Man: Some Remarks on the Alger Stories." *Wisconsin Magazine of History,* XLV (Winter 1961–62), 79–83. Attempts to account psychoanalytically for mutation of Alger the writer into Alger the economic symbol.

Coad, Bruce E. "The Alger Hero." *Heroes of Popular Culture.* Ed. Ray B. Browne et al. Bowling Green, OH: Bowling Green U. Popular Press, 1972. Pp. 42–51. Contends Alger's heroes were obsessed with moneymaking, not virtue.

Cowley, Malcolm. "The Alger Story." *New Republic,* 10 September 1945, pp. 319–20. Valuable comment on Alger's symbolic status; first to question Mayes's authority.

———. "Horatio Alger: Failure." *Horizon,* XII (Summer 1970), 62-65. Best statement of the problem represented by Alger's distortion; flawed by inexplicable praise for Mayes.

Falk, Robert. "Notes on the 'Higher Criticism' of Horatio Alger, Jr." *Arizona Quarterly,* XIX (1963), 151–67. Valuable early bibliographical essay.

Fiore, Jordan D. "Horatio Alger, Jr., as a Lincoln Biographer." *Illinois State Historical Society Journal,* XLVI (1953), 247–53. Fine assessment of Alger's "fair and adequate" Lincoln biography.

Henderson, William. "A Few Words About Horatio Alger, Jr." *Publishers' Weekly,* 23 April 1973, pp. 32–33. Documents Mayes's admission of hoax.

Holland, Norman N. "Hobbling with Horatio, or the Uses of Literature." *Hudson Review,* XII (1959–60), 549–57. Psychological interpretation marred by use of inaccurate biographical data.

Huber, Richard M. *The American Idea of Success.* New York: McGraw-Hill Book Co., 1971. Valuable cultural history; first to document Alger's apparent homosexuality.

Kenner, Hugh. "The Promised Land." *Bulletin of the Midwest Modern Language Association,* VII (Fall 1974), 14–33. Contrasts Alger's and Fitzgerald's versions of the success dream.

Lindberg-Seyersted, Brita. "Three Variations of the American Success Story: The Careers of Luke Larkin, Lemuel Barker, and Lemuel Pitkin." *English Studies,* LIII (April 1972), 125–41. Simple comparisons of Alger's, Howells's, and West's "success stories." Methodologically suspect.

Lynn, Kenneth S. *The Dream of Success.* Boston: Little, Brown, 1955. Uses Alger as touchstone to success theme in Dreiser and London, but overstates.

Mott, Frank Luther. *Golden Multitudes: The Story of Best Sellers in the United States.* New York: Macmillan, 1947. Contains the most reliable statistics on sales of Alger's books.

Nye, Russel. *The Unembarrassed Muse: The Popular Arts in America.* New York: Dial Press, 1970. Excellent summary of Alger's cultural contributions to the late nineteenth century.

Pauly, Thomas H. "*Ragged Dick* and *Little Women:* Idealized Homes and Unwanted Marriages." *Journal of Popular Culture,* IX (1975), 583–92.

Interesting use of Alger to reveal social values of his time, although methodologically suspect.

Rischin, Moses. *The American Gospel of Success: Individualism and Beyond.* Chicago: Quadrangle, 1965. Contains synopsis of *Struggling Upward.*

Scharnhorst, Gary. "The Alger Problem: The Hoax About Horatio Revealed." *BSU Forum,* XV (Spring 1974), 61–65. Discusses the history of the fictionalized Mayes biography and its impact on Alger scholarship.

———. "A Note on the Authorship of Alger's *Life of Edwin Forrest.*" *Theatre Studies,* XXIII (1976–77), 53–55. Reveals Alger's probable collaboration with a cousin in the writing of the authorized biography of the American actor Forrest.

———. "Scribbling Upward: F. Scott Fitzgerald's Debt of Honor to Horatio Alger." *Fitzgerald/Hemingway Annual* (1978), 161–69. Analyzes Fitzgerald's use of Alger in several novels and stories.

———. "A Possible Source for *Sister Carrie:* Horatio Alger's *Helen Ford.*" *Dreiser Newsletter,* IX (Spring 1978), 1–4. Notes parallel between these two works.

Schroeder, Fred. "America's First Literary Realist: Horatio Alger, Jr." *Western Humanities Review,* XVII (1963), 129–37. Argues with some success that Alger anticipated the realistic social fiction of the Gilded Age, but suffers from reliance on inaccurate biographical and sales data.

Seelye, John. "Who Was Horatio? The Alger Myth and American Scholarship." *American Quarterly,* XVII (1965), 749–56. Best critique of the Mayes-Tebbel version of Alger's life and its corruption of Alger scholarship.

Shepard, Douglas H. "Nathanael West Rewrites Horatio Alger, Jr." *Satire Newsletter,* III (Fall 1965), 13–28. Parallels two Alger plots with West's *A Cool Million.*

Shuffelton, Frank. "Bound to Rise—But Not Too Far." *Illinois Quarterly,* XXXIX (Fall 1976), 51–64. A basically sound description of Alger's novels as "recruiting pamphlets for the ranks of middle management."

Tebbel, John. "Horatio Alger, Jr., and the American Dream: From Rags to Riches." *Arts and Sciences,* II (Spring 1963), 17–22. Analyzes Alger's role in Gilded Age America as both a moralist and exponent of social mobility.

Weiss, Richard. *The American Myth of Success.* New York: Basic Books, 1969. One chapter interprets Alger as a "nostalgic spokesman of a dying order."

Wimberly, Lowry Charles. "Hemingway and Horatio Alger, Jr." *Prairie Schooner,* X (Fall 1936), 208–11. Weak attempt to parallel sections of "The Killers" and *Jed the Poorhouse Boy.*

Wohl, R. Richard. "The 'Country Boy' Myth and Its Place in American Urban Culture: The Nineteenth-Century Contribution." *Perspectives in American History,* III (1969), 77–156. Views Alger as exponent of the myth of the virtuous country boy.

————. "The 'Rags to Riches Story': An Episode of Secular Idealism" *Class, Status, and Power: A Reader in Social Stratification.* Eds. Reinhard Bendix and Seymour Martin Lipset. Glencoe, IL: Free Press, 1953. Pp. 388–94. Early attempt to account for Alger's mutation into economic symbol.

Wright, Richard. "Alger Revisited, or My Stars! Did We Read That Stuff?" *PM,* 16 September 1945, magazine section, p. 13. A strongly critical assessment by the eminent black novelist.

Zuckerman, Michael. "The Nursery Tales of Horatio Alger." *American Quarterly,* XXIV (1972), 191–209. Best available critical comment, although limited to "Ragged Dick series."

Index

DATE DUE

DEMCO 38-297